Life Skills
For
Teenage
Boys

Advice on Being More Confident, Dating, Managing Your Money, Dealing With Peer Pressure, Healthy Relationships, and Other Skills

Pathways Press

Publishing.com
helped create and
publish this book.

As a self-publisher, I would like to thank
Publishing.com for their professional assistance
with publishing this book.

Publishing has changed my life, and I would like
to empower my readers with the same
opportunity to reach your dreams, start a side
hustle and earn extra income.

No writing skills required!

Scan this!

JOIN AT
MY.PUBLISHING.COM/PATHWAYSPRESS-LSTB
TODAY AND MAKE PASSIVE INCOME PUBLISHING

Table of Contents

Introduction

There are so many things that I wish I had known as a teenager. Growing up is hard, and the fact of not knowing enough about the world only makes it harder. I wish I knew that everyone is insecure about something and that it is normal to change your mind a lot, so you should keep your options open. I wish I knew how much I didn't know and that the world never revolved around my friends or relationships. I wish someone had told me to find what I loved and explore that, to be kind to others, and that you get what you pay for.

But this isn't about me—it is about you. As you come into the crazy world of being a teenager, there are a lot of things that I bet you do not know, things that would make your life so much easier. Being a teenager is hard, especially if you feel like no one in the world understands your struggles. I'm here to help.

You're experiencing a confusing time in life, one where there are so many things to learn and see. This book will teach you everything you need to know to survive being a teenager and make it into adulthood prepared and ready. You'll learn how to care for your mind and body, how to thrive in school, and more. Ways to connect with others, laundry, and finances will no longer linger in the back of your mind as a great, big question mark. Instead, through this book, you will learn how to navigate these situations, too.

You see, something else no one tells you about being a teenager is that no matter what, it will be hard, but it doesn't have to be that hard. You can make your life so much easier with the right resources, and not to brag, but I think you've found the one! Don't believe me? Let me prove it to you! Dive into this book with an open mind, and see how much you learn and grow by the end of it. Come on! You've got what it takes.

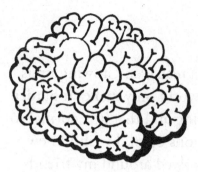

Chapter 1: Building a Strong Mind

A lot of books geared toward teens just like you start with physical health—but this isn't one of those books. We strongly believe that mental health is the key to becoming a strong, well-balanced adult, and as such, we're starting the book there. Mental health is so important when you are a teen. There are a lot of things you are going through, things that adults in your life can't or won't understand. Especially for teens without a strong support network, understanding how to build a strong mind is crucial. With a strong mind, you can handle anything that comes your way. We understand the importance of mental health in and out—you need it to do anything in life. Let's explore the things that you can do to become strong in your mind and take on the real world.

Peer pressure is something that you will undoubtedly face in your teenage years. It is something I went through and something that everyone I know went through as well. Peer pressure often seems like no big deal until it happens to you. It can be one of the most damaging things to your mental health, but developing a strong mind can help you combat peer pressure with ease. You may face peer pressure when it comes to clothes, things you consume, and more, making you stray away from who you are as a person. Right now, you might think that it makes no sense why someone would fall for being peer pressured, but let's dive deeper into what peer pressure is, why it is important to stand up to it, and how you can do so.

THE IMPORTANCE OF STANDING UP TO PEER PRESSURE

I want to tell you a story. Maybe you've heard this one before, and maybe not. It is called "The Emperor's New Clothes," and it is a classic story by famed author Hans Christian Anderson. In this story, two weavers visit a city. Weavers used to be the people responsible for making clothes because, back then, we didn't have the same level of manufacturing that we did today. These weavers entered the town and said that they could make people something really special—clothes that appear to be invisible to stupid people. Naturally, people were jumping at the chance to get these robes and outfits made in such a special way.

Now, of course, this sounds too good to be true. We all know that clothing isn't going to be invisible to stupid people—not really. Maybe in a metaphorical sense, but the weavers had really convinced these people that they would be genuinely invisible to the eye if someone was stupid. After the weavers left and went home, they pretended to make the clothes people had asked for. Yes, pretended because you obviously cannot make invisible clothing. The emperor of this city had asked to be made a suit that would be invisible to the stupid citizens of the city, so this is what they returned to the city with the next day—an invisible suit, or so they told him.

So the next day, the two weavers went back into the city. They had the "suit" that they had made in hand and presented it to everyone in the city. The weavers asked the emperor to wear the suit, and he put on the suit—or at least, he pretended to. Everyone in the city was shocked; they could not see the suit. But because the weavers told them that the suit was invisible only if they were stupid, people began to lie throughout the crowd.

"I can see it! What a splendid suit!" they cried from the crowd.

One after another, people claimed they could see the suit and how marvelous it was.

"He's not wearing anything at all," came from the crowd. A child and his friends began to holler about the fact that there was no suit at all.

Because the kids said something, people began to slip from their stupor, realizing that there was never any suit at all.

DON'T FALL FOR PEER PRESSURE

So, what does this have to do with peer pressure? Well, in order to understand this connection, we first have to understand the message of the story. The message of the story is that you shouldn't agree with others just because you want to appear a certain way. In the story, people began to lie so that they wouldn't be interpreted as stupid. But because they were found out to have lied, they only caused themselves to appear more idiotic in the end.

When it comes to peer pressure, it can make you do things that are, at the end of the day, rather stupid. It can lead to you saying things that do not align with how you really feel, or it can make you think things that you ordinarily wouldn't. I know you are probably tired of hearing about "falling into the wrong crowd," but seriously—peer pressure is the fastest way to do that. Falling into peer pressure can make you lose a part of yourself that you only regain through hard work and overcoming that traumatic experience—yes, peer pressure can be a form of trauma—which is something you have the power to avoid altogether. Not only does avoiding and standing up to peer pressure keep you out of trouble, but it keeps you safe and helps you remain true to yourself. It keeps you from looking stupid, and even if you might not look "cool" for standing up to peer pressure, some things are more important than being cool; you will learn that as we move through this book.

UNDERSTANDING PEER PRESSURE

So, what is peer pressure and why does it occur in the first place? What is and isn't peer pressure, and what encourages people to peer pressure others? These and other questions may be buzzing around in your head right now, but do not worry. I'll answer all of these and more for you, granting you the tools necessary to understand the dynamics that go into peer pressure.

WHAT PEER PRESSURE REALLY IS

Let's start with a definition of what peer pressure is—because, after all, you might know what it feels like to be peer pressured, but having the words to describe something is immensely empowering as well. Peer pressure refers to individuals who belong to the same social group influencing others to do things that they do not want to do or wouldn't ordinarily do (Hartney, 2022). To break that down, think about what it means to be peers with someone. Your peers are people your age with whom you have the opportunity to socialize regularly—people you attend school with, are in clubs or sports with, etc. Therefore, peer pressure occurs when someone within this circle influences you to engage in something you normally wouldn't do if left to your own devices.

THE TYPES OF PEER PRESSURES

Peer pressure is typically used in a negative sense. How often do you hear someone talking about positive peer pressure? I'm willing to bet that it is not often at all. But did you know that peer pressure *can* be positive? Many people do not know this, which is part of why it is so important to understand the three main types of peer pressure: spoken vs. unspoken, direct vs. indirect, and positive vs. negative peer pressure.

Spoken peer pressure occurs when someone says something to you aloud with the intention of influencing you to do something. For example, let's say that your peer is trying to convince you to engage in substance use, something you do not do on your own. Spoken peer pressure might look like them saying to you, "Come on, one time won't hurt."

On the other hand, peer pressure can be unspoken. Unspoken peer pressure occurs when someone feels compelled to do something due to a silent standard set by a crown. For instance, if everyone at a party is using a substance, you might feel peer pressured non-verbally to engage as well.

Similarly, there is such a thing as direct and indirect peer pressure. Direct peer pressure is something that occurs when someone uses either verbal or non-verbal cues in order to convince someone to do something. You might be wondering how this differs from verbal peer pressure. As it turns out, verbal peer pressure is also direct peer pressure, but non-verbal peer pressure can be direct too.

Indirect peer pressure, on the other hand, occurs when no one is trying to convince you of anything, but rather the environment that you are in makes it feel as though you should do something.

Finally, we have to make the distinction between positive and negative peer pressure. Positive peer pressure can occur when someone influences you to engage in a behavior that is beneficial to you in some way. For instance, you can feel peer pressured to do your homework by a study group, which is often a positive form of pressure. Negative peer pressure is different; it occurs when someone influences you in a way that you do not like or isn't good for you. This can include things like drug abuse, sexual encounters, etc.

CAUSES AND EFFECTS OF PEER PRESSURE

Now that you understand the types of peer pressure and what makes each one distinct, it is important to understand what causes peer pressure and the effects that it can have. It can be really easy to allow yourself to be influenced by others, but at the end of the day, this is something you have to learn to resist. Don't worry; I'll teach you how.

In general, though, peer pressure is caused by an overwhelming need to fit in, bolster self-esteem, or avoid rejection. Someone might pressure you because they want company in their bad habits or because they think it is cool to do so. You might allow them to do so because you are afraid of not fitting in with their group.

However, the negative effects associated with peer pressure are worth paying mind to; peer pressure is nothing to take lightly. From mental health concerns like anxiety and depression to life-threatening altercations, peer pressure can truly be a life-ruiner if you allow it to be. Peer pressure can make you lose touch with yourself, spurring these feelings of mental illness, or it can inspire you to do harmful things that put the life of yourself or others at risk. Either way, learning how to overcome and fight against peer pressure is crucial to maintaining a strong mind when it comes to growing up.

CONFIDENCE IS KEY

When it comes to overcoming peer pressure, confidence truly is key. Being able to maintain a degree of confidence, even when facing direct peer pressure, can prevent you from having to deal with some of the more negative aspects that can accompany it. But for a lot of people your age, it can be really hard to understand confidence and harder still to develop it.

WHAT IS CONFIDENCE?

In order to develop something, you first have to understand what it really is—and confidence is no different. What does it mean to have self-confidence? Self-confidence can be defined in many ways. Most simply, I believe that self-confidence involves having the courage to know yourself and act in accordance with what you truly believe. Self-confidence involves feeling positive about yourself in a way that inspires you to act based on what you think is best for you. Some signs that you have a strong level of self-confidence include

- being able to value yourself regardless of your mistakes or shortcomings.

- having the ability to feel good about yourself, even with imperfections.

- understanding that you're inherently worth love and respect, no matter what.

- possessing the courage to stand up for yourself.

- accepting yourself in your entirety.

WHY SHOULD I BE CONFIDENT?

Self-confidence is one of the most important skills that you can develop as a teenager. Just why is that the case, though? Self-confidence connects to every aspect of our life, including the parts that make us feel happy and satisfied with our life. When you have a good level of self-confidence, you are less likely to be prone to anxiety and fear—two emotions that every teenager dreads (Markway, 2018).

Furthermore, a good degree of self-confidence leads to increased motivation. When you have strong confidence in yourself, you are more likely to take risks and steps toward goals that you want to achieve, further motivating you. Self-confidence also boosts your ability to be resilient in the face of adversity, as well as to experience more fulfilling relationships. When it comes to the benefits that self-confidence can provide, not one stone is left unturned.

HOW TO BUILD SELF CONFIDENCE

I understand what you may be thinking; being confident is hard! It can feel impossible to develop a strong sense of self-confidence in a world that seems to have some reason to put us down at all times. But there are definitely a few tips that I can provide that will help you build up your self-confidence. Some ways that you can work to be more confident in yourself include

- refusing to compare yourself to others. Understand that social media and other representations of life online aren't realistic. Remind yourself that comparing yourself to others isn't helping and that life isn't a competition. When you feel jealous of others' lives, remind yourself of your strengths, successes, and things that you have to be grateful for.

- making the active choice to surround yourself with positive individuals. Consider whether your friends make you feel positive or negative. Surrounding yourself with positive people is a great way to influence yourself in a positive manner. Surrounding yourself with positive individuals can help build your confidence because they will naturally want what's best for you.

- caring for your body in various ways. When you feel good about your body, you are able to be more confident. Focus on eating healthy foods, exercising when you can, getting enough sleep, and spending time each day doing something that relaxes you.

- treating yourself with kindness and engaging in positive self-talk. Understand that everyone has weaknesses and times in which they fail, and this is a natural part of life. By being kind to yourself, you improve your ability to be confident in yourself and love yourself despite any flaws that you may perceive yourself to have.

Confidence can go a long way in alleviating some of the effects of peer pressure, but that's not the only tool in your kit for combating peer pressure.

OVERCOMING PEER PRESSURE

When it comes to handling peer pressure, there are a few tips and tricks I have up my sleeve. Confidence isn't something that you build overnight, and as such, you are going to need to understand how to combat peer pressure if confidence isn't enough or if you are still working on developing your self-confidence. With these tips, you are sure to be able to handle any form of peer pressure that is thrown at you.

TAKE YOUR TIME

The first thing you should keep in mind is that you are allowed to take your time. When it comes to a decision, especially one where you are feeling any degree of pressure, understand that it is okay to take your time making a decision. If it feels like someone is pressuring you into doing something you do not really want to do, do not quickly agree to it without thinking. Take a few breaths and think about it carefully.

If someone seems like they want an answer now, tell them you need some time to think about it. If they continue to pressure you for an immediate answer beyond that, tell them that you are being made uncomfortable and would rather be of sound mind when you make a decision. The important thing to remember is that if someone cares about you, they won't pressure you to make an immediate decision if it is clear that you want time to think about it. A good friend will understand.

KNOW YOUR REASONING

It is also important to think about your reasoning for doing something. When you take your time to consider a situation, think about why you actually want to do it. If it is just to seem cool or to fit in, then you are definitely being peer pressured and should reconsider engaging in whatever it is. If your reasoning doesn't have anything to do with what's best for you, then that's a clear indicator that something may be afoot.

OFFER ANOTHER OPTION

Something else that you may want to do is offer an alternative option. For example, if your friend is trying to convince you to do something that you do not want to do or feel uncomfortable doing, suggest something similar that you would be comfortable with. If your friend is trying to pressure you into drinking, for example, and you are really not comfortable with that, try suggesting that you have juice or sodas instead. You can also alternatively suggest going somewhere where drinking isn't involved to hang out instead, letting your friend know that you'd love their company but aren't comfortable with that aspect of it.

PLAN AHEAD

In addition, it is important to prepare ahead of high-pressure situations. It is very common, for example, for someone to feel pressured to engage in actions that they normally wouldn't when at a party. Being at a party can be confusing, especially with so many people doing so many different things. If you know you are going to a party, plan ahead. Come up with an action plan for what you will do if you are being pressured, and even set up a code word with your parents. When you text them that code word, that will be their sign to come and get you, no questions asked. Setting up something like this is a responsible way to manage peer pressure.

SET STRONG BOUNDARIES

You should also work toward developing strong boundaries and removing people from your life if they do not respect those boundaries. Remember that you are young. I'm not saying that to invalidate how you feel; rather, I say that to remind you that you have so much time to make true friends who do respect your boundaries, and you deserve to have friends that treat you right. One of the biggest ways to develop cohesive boundaries is to learn to say "no" when the time comes.

THE ART OF SAYING "NO"

Saying "no" is something that can be rather difficult. Oftentimes, it feels as though a lot of people expect a lot of different things from us, and many of those things aren't necessarily things that align with what we truly want. This is where the power of saying "no" comes into play. Here are some of the best ways that you can say "no" when someone is pressuring you into something you do not want to do:

1. Simply say "no." In some cases, outright saying no without offering an explanation or chance for debate is your best bet, so long as saying "no" is done so in an assertive manner. Don't feel like you owe anyone an explanation, especially if they're someone who tries to convince you to change your mind after you say "no."

2. When you tell someone that you do not want to do something, try offering a reason as to why you think it is a bad idea. You can even blame your parents if you need to. For instance, say that you can't go to a party because you are worried about potentially getting grounded by your parents or that you have a prior obligation.

3. Use humor to de-escalate the situation or change the topic of conversation altogether. Humor is a great way to distract from the point of a conversation. For example, if someone is offering you a substance, you can make a joke about, "Yeah, and then I'm going to go [do something more drastic] afterward," followed by a curt laugh. Oftentimes, this serves as just enough of a distraction to get someone off of your back.

4. Make any excuse to get out of it. Anything from parents like the aforementioned option to appointments or hanging out with a different friend can help you avoid a troublesome situation. I definitely recommend using excuses, particularly with people who do not seem to be willing to accept your boundaries.

5. Suggest that you do something else that you are more comfortable with doing. Your activity may be more fun, and besides, you never know who else is feeling pressured as well. You may be surprised to find that plenty of people would rather do something like watch a movie than go to a party.

6. Ignore the suggestion. Seriously—pretend like you do not even think that the activity is worth dignifying with a discussion. This can establish that you do not think it is cool or fun to engage in pressure-based activities without making yourself seem "uncool" to others.

7. Leave. If someone is continuously asking you to do something that you do not feel comfortable doing, feel free to just leave the situation.

8. Talk to your close friends about how they feel about the situation and see if they perhaps feel the same—chances are that they do.

By learning the power to say no, you can avoid a lot of trouble down the line.

Building a strong mind that is resistant to health-damaging peer pressure is an instrumental part of being a successful teenager and transferring those skills into adulthood. In the next chapter, we'll discuss how to strengthen your body—the other pillar of a strong, healthy teenage body.

Beating the Pressure

Peer pressure is, unfortunately, a normal part of becoming an adult. Listed below are some ways that you can overcome peer pressure. Give an example of a way that you might use each of these skills and successfully beat the pressure.

TAKE YOUR TIME

_____

_____

KNOW YOUR REASONING

_____

_____

OFFER ANOTHER OPINION

_____

_____

PLAN AHEAD

_____

_____

SET STRONG BOUNDARIES

_____

_____

Chapter 2: Maintaining a Strong Body

As a teenager, it can be very easy to let your health and hygiene slip through the cracks. After all, you've got such a busy life with so much going on. If you do not have anyone to help ensure that your hygiene is maintained, you may forget things or straight up not know them in the first place. Then it becomes difficult to maintain a good level of personal health. But personal health is so important as you grow up—not only does it help with your mental health, but you won't feel good if your body isn't in good health.

It might feel like taking care of your physical health is too much. There's so much that goes into our physical health, after all, that it can make it really hard sometimes. To make it easier on you, I've broken physical health down into just three categories that we can explore together: hygiene, fitness, and nutrition. By focusing on these three areas, you can maintain your physical health with ease.

HYGIENE 101

The first thing that we're going to focus on is personal hygiene. Hygiene involves keeping yourself clean inside and out, and it is important for many reasons. Not only does strong personal hygiene keep you in good health, but it gives others a good impression of you too. Let's explore some ways to maintain personal hygiene.

SHOWERING OR BATHING DAILY

Let's be real with each other—how often do you shower? You might be tired of your mom or dad nagging you to shower more often, or you might be surprised by how often it seems like girls shower. But, one boy to another, there is a really good reason to be attentive to showering daily. Well, actually, there are a few reasons. First, showering or bathing on a daily basis helps you smell good. There's a stereotype that goes around saying that boys smell worse than girls, and a lot of that is because boys are prone to avoiding bathing daily. You can defeat this stereotype with a brief shower or bath every day. Even if you can only handle showering every other day, it is still a start that'll do you some good.

Another reason why showering or bathing every day is important is because it helps maintain good skin quality. Over time, dirt and dead skin can accumulate on your body. This can cause things like breakouts, swelling, and other skin damage that no one wants to deal with, especially not as a teen.

The last major reason to shower or bathe every single day is that avoiding showering or bathing can be dangerous. The sweat, germs, and bacteria that accumulate on your body over time need to be washed away. If they're not, they can cause infections, itching, and pain in rather unsavory areas. Therefore, it is important to make sure that you wash yourself daily and wash yourself well.

WASHING YOUR HANDS

Washing your hands is something else that you simply cannot forget to do. A lot of people talk about how important washing your hands is, but they do not cover everything you need to know. For example, can you name five different times in which you are supposed to wash your hands? Most people can only name two or three. In general, you should wash your hands

- after using the restroom.

- after you cough or sneeze.

- before and after touching food.

- before eating.

- after playing with animals.

- after being outside.

- before and after changing your contacts.

And in many other situations. Washing your hands is important to your personal health in that it can ensure that no pathogens are introduced to your own body. It also helps keep other people safe. Wouldn't it be gross to shake someone's hand after they sneezed into it? Yeah, it would. Don't be that person!

BRUSHING YOUR HAIR AND HAIRCUTS

Brushing your hair and getting regular haircuts is another important part of personal hygiene. At least once a day, you should brush through your hair—this helps keep it tangle-free and looking neat. No one has a good impression of someone with tangled and messy hair! If you really want to dedicate yourself to the hair-brushing routine, you should brush your hair before bed and after you wake up, making it a part of what you do to get ready for the day and for bed alike.

It is also important to get your hair cut professionally at least once every three months, even if it is just a trim. Doing so keeps your hair healthy and in tip-top shape, preventing split ends and encouraging the growth of new hair at the same time.

BRUSHING YOUR TEETH

I cannot exaggerate the importance of brushing your teeth twice a day. After our baby teeth fall out, the teeth we have are the ones we're going to carry with us for the rest of our lives. Trust me, the costs associated with dental surgery to repair teeth are no joke. At your age, it is still possible to reverse most damage caused to your teeth, even if you've had poor brushing habits thus far.

Making sure to brush your teeth twice a day is the best way to prevent things like cavities and cracked teeth. If you do not brush your teeth twice a day, then you leave yourself susceptible to things like cavities, cracks, pain, swelling, gingivitis, and more—all things that are costly to fix and avoidable in the first place. Plus, if you brush your teeth, your breath will always smell fresh, giving people a wonderful impression of you!

DON'T FORGET TO FLOSS

Flossing is also an important component of dental hygiene. It is something a lot of people skip out on in their dental routine. After all, isn't brushing enough? As it turns out, you are going to need to do more than just brush your teeth in order to keep them healthy. Flossing gets rid of any build-up between the teeth as well as cleans places that a toothbrush cannot reach easily. Moreover, flossing is good for the health of your gums, which often suffer as a result of poor brushing practices. Flossing regularly, at least once a day, can help keep your breath fresh too.

Ideally, you should floss your teeth at least once a day by moving the floss back and forth between each tooth. If you want, they sell coated floss that tastes great, or you can buy floss picks that make flossing easier on the hands and less time-consuming. I personally favor the picks.

SHAVING

At some point in your teenage years, you are probably going to want to learn how to shave. Shaving can be a bit difficult the first time around, but with the right tips and some practice, the process can become much easier.

First, you need to pick the right razor. Many people like to go for electric razors because of their convenience, but you will quickly find that manual razors have better coverage when it comes to getting a smooth shave. Additionally, it is important that your razor has a clean, sharp blade with at least two blades in the head. Most people prefer razors with a moveable head as well. Always shave with shaving cream. In addition, aftershave is important because it helps rehydrate.

It is also good to know how to deal with cuts and nicks that you may experience when shaving. This is a normal part of shaving and just something everyone has to come to deal with. If you cut yourself while shaving, use a clean tissue or cloth to press against the cut in order to stop the bleeding. Furthermore, if you have a pimple where you need to shave, I recommend either using an electric razor or skipping shaving for a few days; otherwise, you are likely to cut yourself.

And finally, before you start shaving for the first time, here are five steps to doing so that will save you a lot of grief:

1. Wet your face with warm water.

2. Apply shaving cream to your face.

3. Place the razor on the area you want to shave and use short, slow strokes in the direction of hair growth.

4. Do the trickier spots on your face, like near your lips and neck, last and stretch the skin to make a flat surface for shaving where needed.

5. When finished, rinse with cold water and apply aftershave.

You're all set!

NAIL, SKINCARE, AND DEODORANT

Taking care of your skin and nails, as well as understanding how to use various products, is important too. Let's start with basic skincare. Acne, dry skin, and whatever else you may be facing can be really embarrassing as a teen. That's why it is so important to develop a good skincare routine early on. In general, your skincare routine should contain the following:

1. Cleansing with soap or a face wash formulated for your skin type at least twice a day.

2. Moisturizing with an oil-free moisturizer after cleansing.

In addition, it is important that you wash your hands before touching your face to avoid acne. You should also disinfect your cell phone and change your pillowcases regularly!

Next up is nail care. At least once a week, you should trim or file your nails. If they grow slower, then you can probably wait for two weeks or so, but trimming your nails regularly is important. This goes for your toenails as well—something a lot of people often forget to do. Trimming and filing your nails is important for keeping them healthy and looking neat. Trust me, the appearance of your nails matters more than you think! Also, if you feel like getting even more dedicated, adding a thin clear coat of nail polish can help you protect your nails from damage even further. No one will even notice you are wearing it!

Finally, we need to talk about deodorant. People tend to underestimate the power of a simple swipe of deodorant but think about it—how often have your gym coaches, teachers, or parents remarked about the smell of young boys being less than pleasant? I know this was a common course of discussion when I was growing up, and it can easily be remedied with deodorant. I recommend something with 24-hour coverage and a light scent. Apply deodorant after your daily shower or in the morning, depending on your preference, to smell great all day. Remember that if you can smell yourself a little, others can smell you a lot—only you get to choose *what* it is they smell.

CHANGE THAT UNDERWEAR

Maybe it is embarrassing to have to be told to change your underwear, but it is also really important that you actually do so. Underwear collects lots of germs and bacteria throughout the day, and re-wearing the same pair is never okay.

You should own at least enough underwear to get you through between laundry days, and you should put on a fresh pair at least once a day to prevent smells, infections, and more from ruining your day.

AVOIDING BAD HYGIENE HABITS

Lastly, when it comes to hygiene is avoiding some common bad hygiene habits. Some habits that you should avoid include

- ❺ not washing your hands regularly.

- ❺ poor dental hygiene.

- ❺ not covering your mouth while coughing or sneezing.

- ❺ skipping showers or not bathing regularly.

- ❺ not washing your hair frequently.

- ❺ wearing dirty clothes.

- ❺ sharing personal items.

- ❺ not cleaning or changing your bedding regularly.

- ❺ not properly disposing of used tissues or hygiene products.

- ❺ neglecting nail and foot hygiene.

- ❺ poor toilet hygiene.

- ❺ neglecting hand hygiene when preparing or handling food.

- ❺ using expired or contaminated personal care products.

- ❺ not disinfecting commonly touched surfaces.

By avoiding these poor hygiene habits, you will feel much cleaner, be more respected, and will overall have a better life than if these bad hygiene habits invade your life.

KEEPING FIT

The second part of maintaining a strong body involves staying fit. This means getting in enough exercise, even when you do not really feel like doing so. Exercise can be

hard, especially when you have school, friends, chores, etc., but with these tips, exercising and finding what works best for you has just been made much easier!

TYPES OF EXERCISE TO CONSIDER

There are many types of exercise to consider, and I wanted to start off by telling you this because of how many teens I hear saying that exercise is boring or not for them. Exercise is a broad term that includes thousands of different activities; at least one is going to be a fit for you. You can start determining what exercise might be perfect for you by looking at the overarching types of exercise.

First is aerobic exercise. Aerobic exercise is best for keeping your heart and lungs in good shape. By definition, aerobic exercise has to get your heart rate up and keep it there for a certain period of time. Some examples of aerobic exercise include dancing, running, tennis, and boxing. A lot of teens opt to begin with running, so here are a few tips to get you started ("Running Strategies for Children and Teens," n.d.):

- Run with proper form. You should run with a neutral head position and relaxed shoulders, with your back slightly forward and your stomach pulled in. Your feet should hit the ground aligned underneath your hips and your knees should never go above your hip level.

- Set goals for your running training that are realistic.

- Practice often or at least regularly, a few times a week.

- Eat a snack about an hour before running, and drink plenty of water. Avoid sugary drinks and caffeinated beverages, as this can increase dehydration.

- Wear the right shoes. Running shoes should fit your gait and foot shape, and they should be light and breathable.

- Stretch beforehand.

Another type of exercise that you might consider is strength training. Also called resistance training, strength training involves building muscles using weights and other objects. Strength training can give your body a better shape, help with pain and stress management, and so much more. Most often, you will use weights or weight machines to work on strength training. If running or other aerobic exercises aren't your speed, I definitely recommend looking into strength training!

The third major type of exercise to think about trying for yourself is bone strengthening—something that a lot of people neglect to think about. Bone strengthening activities place force upon the bones to help keep them strong, which is especially important in your teenage years. If you do not exercise growing up, it is easy for your bones to become brittle and non-functional. Exercises like gymnastics, basketball, and other sports can really make a difference when it comes to bone strength.

I recommend giving each type of exercise a shot before excluding it. There are literally thousands of exercises out there, and one of them is bound to suit you—if not one from each category. The benefits of exercise include a long life, health, energy, and much more. Developing a good exercise habit as a teen is a fantastic way to set yourself up for success.

STARTING A HOME WORKOUT ROUTINE

You do not have to go to the gym to stay in shape. Not only is it costly, but going to a gym can feel awkward when you first start out. It is much easier for teens like you to start with a home workout routine and then transition to the gym when and if the time is right. What you are going to want to do is work out at least three days a week, and across all three of those days, you will want to hit all of the following areas at least once: back, chest, traps, shoulders, triceps, biceps, quads, and hamstrings.

A good sample workout routine might look like this:

- 10 burpees
- 30 air squats
- one minute plank
- 10 dips
- 10 elevated pike pushups
- repeat the whole thing again

FITNESS TIPS

To finish off your fitness education, I have a few tips that may help you! First and foremost, it is always a good idea to set an exercise goal. What is it you hope to accomplish by exercising? Some people opt for "health," while others opt for "weight loss" as their goal, for example. Having a goal in mind helps you know if you are on the right track, making sure that your efforts are not in vain. Goals are the most important aspect of exercise, in my opinion. They will keep you motivated.

Also, make sure that you spend some time in nature when it comes to exercising. It can be really tempting to shut yourself in and spend all of your time indoors when it comes to exercise, but something as simple as taking a walk around the block has proven health benefits when it comes to stress and anxiety. Spending a little bit of time outside each week is really great for you!

In addition, make sure that you do not overwork yourself. It might be tempting to spend all of your time exercising when you first start out, thinking that you will make more progress toward your goals that way. But in reality, if you overwork yourself, then the efforts that you've made won't pay off. This is because your body needs time to rest between workouts in order for the work you did to actually "count." It is like sleeping after studying—the brain needs time to consolidate and process that information and it does so by sleeping. Similarly, the body processes workouts on rest days.

Above all, remember that exercising doesn't have to be perfect so long as you are giving it your best shot. Starting any new routine can take a while to get the hang of, but the more you exercise, the easier it'll become and the more your efforts will show!

EATING RIGHT

The last of the three aspects of maintaining a strong body is making sure that you eat right. Even if you have good hygiene and work out, not eating the right food can ruin all of your efforts. A lot of teenagers simply opt to eat snack foods and processed "junk food," but if you take charge of your health by eating right early on, you will thank yourself for it later!

HEALTHY FOOD CHOICES

The first important thing is to make healthy food choices. That's not to say that you can never have your favorite snack; in fact, I encourage you to do so! But it has to be in balance with everything else you eat in order for you to maintain a solid level of health. But what does it mean to make healthy food choices?

In general, you should eat meals that are well-balanced in fruits, veggies, proteins, dairy, and carbs. You should eat three meals a day, and your snacks should be healthy. When you drink things, you should drink mostly water with juice, soda, and other beverages, being limited to one a day. In addition, it is best to opt for baked food instead of fried food, as fried foods contain a lot of unhealthy fats. Also, chicken is better for you than beef, so try to eat chicken when you can. Avoiding processed foods will be your best friend as well.

DIET PLAN EXAMPLE

There are lots of different things that go into having a healthy diet. That's why I've devised an example of a healthy diet plan that you might follow so that you can see what I mean. Of course, you do not have to follow my plan exactly—making your own is going to ensure that you follow it and enjoy it too!

One example of a healthy diet plan could be:

- Two cups of fruit a day.

- Three cups of vegetables a day.

- Eight ounces of grains a day.

- Six to seven ounces of protein a day.

- Three cups of dairy a day.

Also, what you need to eat within a day is going to depend heavily on your body and the amount of calories that you need. Calories are a number that represents the amount of energy food has. Someone who plays sports and works out five days a week is going to need more calories than someone who is relatively sedentary, for example. It is important, therefore, to do your research and talk to your doctor about what healthy eating might look like for you.

HEALTHY EATING HACKS

Finding the opportunity to eat healthy every day can be hard. It is honestly time-consuming and not very fun, especially at first. That's why finding hacks for healthy eating are so important! Some hacks that I think you'd like for healthy eating include:

- Avoid processed foods and swap them out for fresh fruit and veggies when possible.

- Be realistic in your eating goals. Don't expect everything to change overnight, and do not force yourself to believe that your favorite foods are "bad." There are no good and bad foods, only good and bad eating habits.

- Never shop on an empty stomach—you will be more prone to buy what you want at the moment than what you need. Always shop with a list for the same reason.

- Keep lots of healthy snacks around—including in your room and backpack! That way, there is no excuse for eating processed snacks on a whim.

- Slowly work to swap unhealthy foods out—like sugary snacks—for healthier alternatives.

- Eat slower and drink more water. Our stomachs are usually slow at telling us when we're full. By slowing down your eating process, you avoid overeating.

ON MISLEADING FOOD LABELS

The last food tip I want to leave you with is to watch out for misleading food labels. You might've always thought that you could trust what's on the packaging of your food, but that's not always the case! Some food labels can actually be very misleading, causing you to make unhealthy food decisions without knowing any better. Some labels that you should be wary of, as they are often flat-out lies, include labels that tout immunity boosting, fat-free, "light," "made with real fruit," etc. It is always important to look at the actual ingredient labels before trusting anything you buy—and a little additional research can't hurt either.

It is important to be well-rounded. Now that we've covered the mind and body, let's dive into how we can build a smarter you!

FOOD GROUPS

Eating healthy to stay fit isn't just about eating less, but what you eat matters just as much. It is recommended to eat a certain amount of servings from five different food groups. Below, next to a food item from each group, list how many servings per day is recommended.

Chapter 3: Acing Your Academics

The next thing that we simply have to talk about is your academics. Boring, boring, I know. But the truth is that academics are, at this point in your life, your gateway to success. You're young enough that you can do anything you want to in life, but one of the biggest gatekeepers to success is academia. If you do badly in school, you might not be able to get where you want to in life. School only lasts a few years, which makes a convincing argument for trying to do well while it lasts.

What's more, is that everybody loves intelligence. It looks impressive in conversation, at work, and in romantic situations, making you a standout candidate no matter the situation. It is important to boost your brain with intelligence, and acing academics is the best way to do this. Imagine how impressed everyone would be if you took the opportunity to give your grades a 180, completely succeeding in school. Let's talk about some of the things that can make this your reality.

TIME MANAGEMENT TECHNIQUES

It never feels like there is enough time when you are a teenager. Competing priorities alongside wanting to do anything but school can make it really hard to manage time responsibly. According to psychologists, educators, and students themselves, however, there are a handful of methods that you can use to elevate your time management techniques. And actually, having good time management leads to *more* free time, not less—so let's find out how you can optimize time and amplify your free time!

THE PARETO PRINCIPLE

Also referred to as the 80/20 rule, the Pareto principle states that 20% of our actions are responsible for 80% of our outcomes. This means that when you have a problem, there is a way to narrow down actions to deal with the most issues at once. You can do this by doing the following:

1. Make a list of all of the major problems that you are facing. This can be anything in any area of life.

2. List out the reasons for each problem; try to truly get to the root cause of a situation.

3. Score each problem based on how much of a problem it is. Give bigger problems bigger numbers.

4. Group your problems together by what has caused them. Then, tally up the score for each group. The group with the highest score is what you are going to work on first.

From there, you are going to try and address whatever the root cause of an issue is. If, for example, your grades are slipping due to social media being a distraction, think about what you can do to fix that. This method works best for those who are thinkers and analytics by nature, but if that's not you, do not worry! There are plenty of other methods you can use.

THE POMODORO TECHNIQUE

This is one of my favorite methods for getting things done. The Pomodoro method uses intervals to break work down into shorter periods, ultimately helping you get more done. The method works quite simply. Choose a task that you need to get done, like a homework assignment or studying. Set a timer for about 20 or 25 minutes, and work for that duration of time. When the timer goes off, set a 5-minute timer for a break where you do something unrelated to your work. Repeat this process three more times, then take a longer, 30-minute break. Keep going until you are done!

This method works best for people who experience burnout or are heavily creative. If you work best with technological aids, there are plenty of apps that can help you time yourself, such as Pomodoro and Forest. Some apps even lock features of your phone to minimize distractions.

THE EISENHOWER MATRIX

Former President Dwight Eisenhower was a member of the army before he took office. He invented his matrix to rank events based on their urgency and importance. The matrix looks something like this (University of St. Augustine for Health Sciences, 2019):

	Urgent	Not urgent
Important	Do. These are tasks that are important and need to be done immediately, such as a pressing chore or schoolwork.	Decide. These are tasks that are important, like working out or spending time with friends, but not urgent. You can decide whether or not you need to do these on an individual basis.
Not important	Delegate. These are urgent tasks that aren't important– things that are time sensitive but have no real impact if they do not get done.	Delete. These are things that aren't urgent or important, like social media or goofing off.

To use the matrix, draw a similar four-by-four square on a piece of paper and sort events as necessary. The idea is that you work on important tasks and either delegate or remove non-important tasks. Or at least you should do the important ones first. This is a good way to help prioritize your life when you have things that are conflicting.

PARKINSON'S LAW

Parkinson's law describes a phenomenon that exists around how long it takes us to do a task. It states that the amount of time you give yourself to complete a task is how much time you will need to complete it. For example, if you tell yourself it is going to take two hours to study, then it will take two hours, even if it would've only taken 45 minutes had you not set that limit for yourself.

The idea behind using Parkinson's law is that you shouldn't give yourself more time than necessary. In order to follow Parkinson's law, you have to avoid giving yourself extraneous time; in fact, get into the mindset that you should do things as fast as possible while maintaining quality in your work. Don't worry about keeping an eye on the clock. Some ways that you can work to implement Parkinson's law include:

- Working without a laptop charger. This has you in a race against the clock to get your work done, which can be quite a fun way to get through an arduous assignment.

- Setting deadlines earlier than the real deadlines. If you have an assignment due at midnight, charge yourself to get it done by 4 p.m., for instance.

- Tell yourself that after x amount of time, you are done—even if you do not get finished. Use the opportunity to take a break!

Parkinson's law can absolutely help you get through tasks without wasting unnecessary time.

TIME BLOCKING

Another method that you can use is the time-blocking method. Time blocking involves a method where you break your day into times based on tasks. You do it like this:

1. Take a piece of paper and divide it in half. On the left side of the paper, write down hours of time in intervals, even breaking it down to a half hour if you'd like.

2. Estimate how long each task will take you and schedule it on the right.

3. Leave time for adjustments that may need to be made throughout the day.

This will help you see what you have to do throughout the day as well as how long you have to complete each thing.

THE GETTING THINGS DONE METHOD

The Getting Things Done method is a wonderful method for breaking tasks that you have to complete down into actionable steps that allow you to actually complete what you need to do. You can employ the Getting Things Done method with these steps:

1. Write down the tasks that you need to do, including anything that you find to be particularly pressing. If you need to, you can combine this method

with other methods like the Eisenhower matrix to truly narrow priorities down.

2. Clarify each task. Is it something you can currently do right now? If not, discard it for later.

3. Organize your tasks. Prioritize your tasks in order to what you need to get done based on urgency/time sensitivity.

4. View your list of tasks to view your next priority, and cross off things that you've completed.

5. Contrary to what you might think you should do, start with the smallest tasks first. These are tasks you can get done immediately and cross off of your plate. Then, move on to urgent tasks.

This method helps you get things done as fast and efficiently as possible.

THE RAPID PLANNING METHOD

The rapid planning method is effective for focusing on a goal and accomplishing it. It goes like this:

1. Write down everything that you need to get done this week.

2. Group your tasks together based on what they have in common, such as school-related tasks or chores being grouped based on those criteria.

3. Make three columns on a sheet of paper: one for a task, one for the result you are anticipating from the task, and one for the reason why you are completing the task. List the actions that it takes to get those tasks accomplished.

4. Create an empowering role for yourself—such as star student or stellar studier—anything that gets you excited about your task.

THE PICKLE JAR THEORY

The pickle jar theory helps you sort out what is and is not useful within your daily life (University of St. Augustine for Health Sciences, 2019). Imagine a pickle jar full of sand, pebbles, and then larger rocks. At the bottom is the sand, and at the top are the rocks. The sand represents anything that can disrupt your daily life, like social media, for example. The pebbles are non-urgent tasks that are important and need to be completed, and the rocks are important tasks you simply have to get done today.

Think about how everything you plan to do in a day classifies as either sand, pebbles, or a rock, and estimate how long things will take you to complete in order of rocks to sand. It is a good idea to think about a day in terms of 8–10 hours and leave 6–8 hours of that time unplanned for reorganizing if needed as the day progresses.

EAT THE FROG TECHNIQUE

Finally, we have The Eat The Frog method. The Eat The Frog method is inspired by a quote that says that if you have to choke down a frog, do it at the beginning of the day—that way, everything else you do that day will be easier than eating the frog. This translates to doing the hardest thing that you have to do first, making the rest of your day that follows much easier.

STUDY SMARTER, NOT HARDER

Time management is an important aspect of acing academics, but so is studying smart. Studying hard doesn't necessarily mean that you will gain anything from it, which is why it is so important not just to study but to study well. With these tricks in your toolbox, you're certain to be able to study smarter and not harder.

THE SQ3R METHOD

The SQ3R method is a method that helps with reading comprehension, especially when it comes to reading textbooks, something you undoubtedly do a lot of in your studies. The SQ3R method outlines five steps for reading more effectively (Mozafaripour, 2020):

1. **Survey**. Don't start by reading the whole book; instead, skim the chapter and take notes on headings, images, and other features of the text that stand out.

2. **Question**. Ask yourself questions about the contents of the chapter, such as what the chapter might be about and what you already know.

3. **Read**. Read the full chapter and try to answer any questions you jotted down from the last step.

4. **Recite**. Once you've finished a section, summarize it in your own words.

5. **Review**. After finishing the chapter, review the material by quizzing yourself and rereading as needed.

This method is known for boosting reading comprehension and can make your study sessions way more fruitful.

RETRIEVAL PRACTICE

Retrieval practice is a fancy term for remembering what you've learned at a later time. Practicing retrieval of information, meaning trying to recall what you studied, is going to let you know what you truly know and what you may need to brush up on. You can practice retrieval in a few ways. First, use practice tests to quiz yourself. Many are online for free and are very useful. Second, you can make up your own questions and test yourself on the topic. Finally, using flashcards is an awesome method for retrieval that can make a world of difference. I recommend using Quizlet or physical notecards to help you with this.

SPACED PRACTICE

Spaced practice is a study technique that encourages you to study over a more extended period of time instead of cramming right before something important (University of St. Augustine for Health Sciences, 2019). Spacing out the time frame in which you study makes your brain remember the information better, building up stronger connections to the material. It is important to give yourself at least three days to study any concept for this reason. It might sound much easier to just cram the material, but trust me—spaced practice is one of the most effective methods out there and it truly makes a difference!

THE FEYNMAN TECHNIQUE

Next up, we have the Feynman technique. This technique is designed to help you learn different concepts quicker by explaining them in simple terms. In order to try this method, you need to get out a sheet of paper. Write down the subject or topic at the top of the paper, and below that, explain it in your own words like you were teaching the concept to someone with no prior knowledge. After that, you can go over what you wrote and see where you made any mistakes, correcting and simplifying as you go.

THE LEITNER SYSTEM

The Leitner system is a system of learning something with flashcards (University of St. Augustine for Health Sciences, 2019). You're going to need five "boxes," which do not actually have to be boxes; you can just put the cards in piles. These boxes are used to keep track of when you need to study each set. Every card starts in the first box and moves to the next one once it is mastered. If you get a card wrong, you move it back a box. Box one has to be studied daily, and box two every other day. Box five gets studied every two weeks.

COLOR CODED NOTES

Color-coded notes are great to help you remember what you learned in a way that is both effective and fun at the same time. Studies show that color coding your notes can help improve the rates of retention and memory you have when it comes to a topic (Mozafaripour, 2020). Because of this, it is a good idea to always color-code your notes with a consistent system that you can rely on every time. This can be done with colored pens, highlighters, sticky notes, etc. The best way to develop a color coding system is to assign one color to key points, another to important info, one to dates if you are working on history, etc. Don't make your whole note page light up like Times Square, though—that defeats the purpose of making things stand out with color.

MIND MAPPING

Mind mapping is another great way to help you memorize new concepts and take stock of what you already know, especially if you are a visual learner. The idea is that you create a visual "map" representing everything you know about a topic. You can create a mind map by taking a blank piece of paper and writing your topic in the middle. Circle it, box it in, or do whatever you want with it; mind maps can absolutely look fun! Once you've done that, connect your main ideas to the middle circle, and connect sub-topics for those new circles. This will help you see how everything is connected and what you can do to improve your learning.

GOAL SETTING

When it comes to your academics, it is a good idea to have some goals laid out that tell you what you hope to accomplish. But it is not good enough to just set any old goal—no, there are certain methods you can follow to make your goals effective, memorable, and functional, too. Although, you may be wondering why you should set goals in the first place.

Setting goals for your academics is a good idea primarily because it gives you an objective idea of what you want to accomplish with a time constraint telling you by when it must be accomplished. This is a good thing because setting goals allows you to monitor progress; if you are moving too slowly, you know how you need to adjust your initial goal and what you can reasonably expect of yourself. In general, there are a number of impactful and useful methods for goal setting that I'll take you through, allowing you to pick the best one for you.

SMART GOALS AND SMARTER GOALS

SMART goal setting is one of the most popular goal-setting methods to date. The acronym SMART stands for specific, measurable, achievable, realistic, and time-sensitive, each of the criteria contributing something unique to how your goal plays out successfully. Let's look at how SMART goals break down:

- **Specific**: Your goal has to be clearly defined and intentional, something that isn't just a broad idea. For example, setting a goal to study is good, but setting a goal to study lesson three of your bio notes is great.

- **Measurable**: For your goal to be SMART, it has to be measurable. Think about it in terms of the biology studying example. Making that goal measurable would be something like, "I will study my notes until I can recall 75% of lesson three's content without checking my notes."

- **Achievable**: You have to set goals that are objectively accomplishable in order for it to be a SMART goal. There is nothing SMART about setting unachievable goals.

- **Realistic**: Your goal has to be something that you yourself can actually do. For example, it may be possible for someone to master AP biology in a month, but is that something that you can do given your time and competing priorities? Probably not.

- **Time-sensitive**: You have to put a time limit on your goal; otherwise, you can keep pushing it back without consequence. As such, you might have to say that you will accomplish your goal within x amount of days, for example.

That's everything that makes up a SMART goal, but more recently, people have started adding in two more letters to make SMARTER goals—E and R. The E and R stand for evaluate and readjust:

- **Evaluate**: Consider the progress you've made in your goal after a reasonable amount of time to see if you are making good movement forward.

- **Readjust**: Be flexible enough to change things in your goal as needed, like the time it takes or what you can accomplish in a fixed amount of time if you genuinely see a need to do so.

SMART goals are the most effective goal-setting method, in my opinion, making every goal that you set with these criteria one of extreme success.

HARD GOALS

HARD goals aren't goals that are really difficult to do—it is another acronym representing an option you have for steps to set a goal that will succeed. A HARD goal is one that is:

- **Heartfelt**: You need to be able to connect to your goal in a meaningful and emotional way in order for it to be something that you actually accomplish.

- **Animated**: Imagine what your life would be like after you achieve your goal in order to breathe life into it.

- **Required**: Either your goal has to be something necessary for you, or it has to be able to connect to something necessary; otherwise, you may not be motivated to actually achieve your goal.

- **Difficult**: It doesn't have to be a hard thing to do, just something that pushes you in a positive way!

This can be a much friendlier option if SMART goals do not really resonate with you.

WOOP GOALS

Another alternative method of goal setting is the WOOP goal, which I find to be whimsical and fun. WOOP goals follow this format:

- **Wish**: Your goal is a wish; make it one that's exciting for you.

- **Outcome**: Imagine the best possible result that can occur once you achieve your goal.

- **Obstacle**: Consider anything that may slow you down when you try to achieve your goal.

- **Plan**: Plan to circumvent these obstacles if they arise.

This method works particularly well if you are someone who gets bogged down by all of the "what if" questions that play a role in accomplishing your goal.

OKR GOALS

OKR stands for "objectives and key results," which is a common goal-setting device for companies or large groups of people. But you can absolutely use this method on your own if it feels right for what you are working on. In order to work with OKR goals, choose a goal that you want to achieve and lay out the steps that it'll take to get there. These represent smaller goals that lead you to your key results. As you engage with these goals, reevaluate them as needed to keep yourself going in the right direction.

MICRO GOALS

Another option that you have for goal setting when it comes to your academics is micro goals. Micro goals are smaller goals that you set in order to achieve a bigger goal, which can play into any one of the methods we've talked about thus far. A lot of people like micro goals because they help break things down into more manageable bite-sized pieces, creating less overwhelming goals out of one big goal.

When you set your goals for your academic endeavors, choosing one or more of these goal-setting options is bound to lead you right to success. You've got this!

BEATING THE STRESS

Dealing with stress can be one of the most difficult aspects of balancing academics. With anywhere from four to eight classes going at once, it can be really hard to keep up with everything and feel like you still have time for a personal life. That's why it is so important to be able to not just identify stress but to know how to combat it too.

SIGNS OF STRESS

Let's start by talking about the signs that you are stressed out. The signs of stress can differ from person to person, but generally, there are a few that you are going to want to look out for. Some of the most common signs of stress include (Morin, 2020)

- ❂ headaches and stomachaches.

- ❂ issues with sleeping.

- ❂ struggling to focus in school.

- ❂ increased issues with irritability.

- ❂ changes in social patterns.

- ❂ getting sick often.

- ❂ low self-esteem or engaging in negative self-talk.

- ❂ increased worrying.

If you are experiencing multiple of these signs of stress, then it may be necessary for you to take measures that allow you to chill out. How can we do this? Let's find out!

STRESS MANAGEMENT TECHNIQUES

Stress is one of the most common issues that people experience, especially in modern society. You aren't alone in what you are going through, and one of the fortunate aspects about stress being so common is that the solutions are equally as common. Understanding how to minimize stress can be good for you, inside and out.

BREATHING TECHNIQUES

The first way that you can work to manage stress is with solid breathing techniques. Breathwork can help calm the nervous system and increase the sense of calm you feel throughout your whole body. There are hundreds—if not thousands—of breathing techniques available to you. Allow me to guide you through the steps of my personal favorite method:

1. Sit or stand in a relaxed position, and allow your breathing to settle into a rhythm that feels natural for you.

2. Breath deep into your belly without forcing it, letting your stomach expand with the air and contract with your exhales.

3. Breathe in through your nose and out through your mouth as you do so, and repeat this for at least five minutes.

GUIDED MEDITATION

Guided meditation is another excellent option for relaxation when you feel a tad too stressed out. Meditation is a stress relief and coping tool that involves increasing your awareness of yourself or your mind for a set period of time. I could guide you through a meditation myself, but there are so many ways to meditate that no one method works best for everyone. Therefore, I highly recommend searching for "guided meditation for stress" videos online and picking the ones that you like the best to use over and over. Most people who meditate experience the most benefits after keeping at it consistently for three weeks, so give the practice some time before abandoning it!

CREATING A STRESS MANAGEMENT PLAN

I also want to talk with you about setting up a stress management plan. Your stress management plan should incorporate all of the following elements, allowing you to handle stress in a manner that is healthy and effective:

ADDRESS THE PROBLEM

- What is the problem? In other words, what is the culprit causing you to feel stressed out right now? Identify it in words and then address it.

- Take precautions to avoid things that stress you out wherever possible.

- Make a list of all the things you "need" to do, and eliminate things that you can, even if you do not want to do so. Minimizing the amount of things you have to do is the best way to limit stress.

TAKING CARE OF YOUR BODY

- Exercise is, believe it or not, one of the best ways to relieve stress. Getting your body up and moving can be very calming and help you physically shake out the stress that you may be feeling.

- Eat well. Your body can combat illness and feelings of stress when it has all of the nutrients that it needs in order to do so successfully.

- Get enough sleep. If you are sleep deprived, you are going to feel more stressed out, and it only gets worse the older you get—take it from me.

- Relax on purpose. Don't just allow yourself to watch TV or something; rather, make an active attempt to relax without forcing yourself to do anything at all.

DEAL WITH EMOTIONS

- Creating a safe space in your mind is one of the best ways to handle particularly stressful emotions. It gives you somewhere to escape to when you are not feeling well. Create your mental safe haven by imagining a perfect location—one that doesn't already exist to you—and visiting it as much as you need to.

MAKE THE WORLD A BETTER PLACE

- Contribute to the world in some way, either in your daily life or by volunteering. It'll make life less stressful for you.

EXTRACURRICULAR ACTIVITIES

The last thing that I want to talk to you about when it comes to academics is your extracurricular activities. Extracurricular activities are everything you do outside of normal school hours, like clubs and volunteering. Extracurricular activities are something you definitely shouldn't ignore. They make you more well-rounded and prove to be immensely beneficial down the line!

WHY SHOULD I HAVE EXTRACURRICULARS?

Extracurriculars are important for a few reasons. They help you look more impressive to college and prospective employers, sure, but that's not even the best part of engaging in extracurriculars. Extracurricular activities help you build friendships and connections, as well as gain skills that you are going to use for your whole life (like time management and problem-solving skills). In addition, activities like this can help you learn something new and find your true passions in life, all while helping you build confidence in yourself. Even if you think you know what you like already, it is never too late to add some new things to your repertoire.

FINDING THE RIGHT ACTIVITY FOR YOU

There are so many different extracurricular activities out there that it might seem hard to find the right one for you. You can choose the best activity for you by looking in newspapers, online, or through your school for activities that are geared toward your existing interests. You can also consider what type of extracurricular that you might be interested in order to help you narrow it down. Some examples of extracurricular activities include music, STEM, sports, and academic groups.

BALANCING SCHOOL AND EXTRACURRICULARS

A lot of teens feel like it is really difficult to balance the time they spend on schoolwork with their time doing extracurriculars. It is a fair concern, which is why I have some tips to help you mitigate it:

- Put your academics first. At the end of the day, they're called "extra" curriculars for a reason; they're meant to be extra activities that you perform after all of your other obligations are complete. If you feel like you do not have enough time for everything, put academics first.

- Be super selective with what extracurriculars you do. It is easy to overschedule yourself with interesting clubs and activities, but by being selective, you can funnel your time into things you truly care about instead of spreading yourself thin.

- Create a schedule and stick to it. Schedule out study time, extracurricular time, and social time, leaving a bit of time for leeway, and stick to that schedule at all costs.

This chapter talked all about how you can maintain a strong academic life that helps you truly ace your academics. Let's keep moving forward and talk about something else that's important to succeeding in the teenage years: understanding relationships and social media.

SET YOUR GOALS

If you need help setting your goals, this worksheet is perfect for allowing you to do so. Answer each question to the best of your ability, and by the end of it, you will have a concise and effective goal to shoot for.

MY STRENGTHS ARE:

_____

_____

_____

MY WEAKNESSES ARE:

_____

_____

_____

SOMETHING I WANT TO IMPROVE IS:

_____

_____

_____

I WILL IMPROVE IT BY:

_____

_____

_____

POTENTIAL OBSTACLES AND WAYS TO OVERCOME THEM INCLUDE:

_____

_____

_____

I WILL COMPLETE THIS GOAL BY:

_____

_____

_____

Chapter 4: On Dating, Friends, and Social Media

One of the hardest things that you will have to deal with as a teenager is your relationships with others, and the only other thing that compares to this is navigating social media. Both can be really tricky and confusing terrains, which is why it is so important to understand how to navigate each one. Let's jump right into exploring how you can maintain one kind of relationship: friendship.

MAKING FRIENDS

It can be hard to make friends, even as a teenager. You might feel like no one wants to be your friend or that you are not a good enough friend, or you might have hesitations about approaching and maintaining relationships—and that's okay! I'll talk with you about it and demystify everything that comes along with friendship for teens.

THE QUALITIES OF A GOOD FRIEND

Think of the perfect friend. What are some qualities that they have that set them apart from anyone else? Chances are, you have some specific traits in mind or maybe even a specific person, someone who's a really good friend to you. But you know what's just as important as having a good friend? Being a good friend.

Being a good friend is important for so many reasons, but chiefly among them is the fact that it helps you build strong and long-lasting relationships with people who care for you. Those traits you thought of in a good friend are likely to be traits that others look for in you; if you have none of those traits, then people will pass you over for friendship. Why would you be friends with someone who has no good friendly qualities?

Fortunately, it is not too hard to be a good friend, even if you do not have any experience with it! Being a good friend lies in the qualities that define what a good friend truly is. Here are some qualities that you can work on developing in order to be a better friend, and what you should look for in the perfect friend too ("How Teens Can Be and Pick a Good Friend," 2011):

- **Honesty.** A good friend is one who tells the truth, even if the truth isn't what we want to hear at the moment.

- **Interesting.** Good friends are going to be interesting because they share interests with us.

- **Attentive.** Someone who is a good friend listens to their friends and notices things about them, learning whatever they can about their friend to strengthen the bond.

- **Supportive.** Good friends make you feel good about who you are without judgment, and they provide a shoulder to lean on when times get hard.

- **Compassionate.** Caring people make the best friends.

- **Loyal.** Even if you make a mistake, a good friend will be there for you to help you grow.

- **Accepting.** True friends won't try to change who you are.

- **Forgiving.** If you hurt your friend by accident, your friend being forgiving is a sign that they're there for the long run.

By looking for these qualities in others and working to develop them within yourself, you can become a much better friend to others—someone who people will flock to!

TIPS FOR MAKING FRIENDS

You know that phrase about how we can be lonely in a crowded room? It seems that that phrase never feels truer than in high school. Even though the halls are filled with roaming teens, it can be hard to find people to be friends with. If you are struggling to make friends as a teen, here are some things that you can try to improve your chances of making a life-long friend ("5 Simple Tips to Make Friends," 2015):

- Be yourself. Remember that I said a good friend would like you authentically and won't try to change you. Plus, being someone you are not can be very tiring. Just be who you are and friends who are worth your time will be drawn to you.

- ✪ Be open to trying new things. Some of the best bonding experiences happen when people try new things. Be open to new interests, hobbies, and other activities that can help you meet people and get closer to people that you already know.

- ✪ Find opportunities to strike up a conversation. You can use conversations or even extend a compliment to begin a conversation. It might feel awkward, but people love to be asked about themselves and their interests; use this knowledge to your advantage.

- ✪ If you find out that you have an interest in common with someone, find an opportunity to explore that interest together.

- ✪ Go out of your way to stay in touch with potential friends, even if it just involves shooting them a text.

- ✪ By following these tips, I promise you will find it a bit easier to meet true and genuine friends.

SPOTTING TOXIC FRIENDS

Toxic friends are such a bummer. It is, unfortunately, something that nearly every teen has to deal with. Not everyone is self-aware, nor is everyone concerned with being a good friend in the first place. To minimize the harm that a toxic friend is able to cause you, it is important to be able to notice the signs of a toxic friend as early as possible. Here are a handful of signs that may indicate that you are in a toxic friendship:

- ✪ They do not respect your boundaries. Someone who repeatedly breaks or ignores your boundaries, including pushing the line of them further and further, is someone who is behaving toward you in a toxic manner.

- ✪ Someone who always needs something from you is someone that you should watch out for. Someone who is a toxic friend will expect constant support and will then make you feel guilty if you say "no." This is toxic behavior.

- ✪ If someone refuses to take accountability if they hurt you, that's a sign that this is someone who is exhibiting toxic behavior.

- Weaponizing struggles is something that you are going to have to look out for as well. Determining if someone is weaponizing their struggles may be a bit difficult, but generally, weaponizing struggles will be guilting you into doing something for or with them on account of an issue they're going through. This extends beyond supporting a friend, going right into toxic territory.

- A toxic friend might try to make you feel guilty for spending time with other people.

- They dismiss your beliefs. Someone who invalidates what you believe in or value is automatically a bad friend, especially if you've talked to them about this and they continue to do it.

HOW TO HANDLE A TOXIC FRIEND

Depending on what you hope to come out of the situation, there are a few ways you can handle a toxic friendship. The first thing to do is to determine what you can and cannot control about the situation and that you make sure to be respectful even if they aren't respecting you. By being disrespectful, a toxic person will consider it to be an excuse to treat you poorly.

One of the biggest things to do when dealing with a toxic person is to handle things when they happen. In other words, do not let things fester; if your friend upsets you or treats you poorly, confront them right away. Send a text or speak to them in person, letting them know that what they did wasn't okay or that they cannot do that to or with you. If they violate your privacy online, send them a private message asking them to take down whatever they posted.

In some situations, though, this might not work, and a larger conversation may be necessary. Talk to them about how you feel, and try to phrase things in terms of your emotions instead of saying "you did" or "you always," as these kinds of statements can seem like an accusation and make the other person respond with hostility.

It is also a good idea to set new and stronger boundaries after having a conversation like this. You may need to reduce contact or take a break from the person in order to ensure that these boundaries are respected, and that's perfectly fine to do.

DATING

Ah, one of the most troublesome parts of being a teen! When it comes to dating, there are undoubtedly a lot of questions you have that no one is going to answer for you… until now, that is. Dating as a teen doesn't have to be scary. Learn how to avoid tricky situations with this advice for navigating your romantic life as a teen.

DATING DO'S AND DON'TS

Let's start with a quick rundown of the dos and don'ts associated with dating as a teen, starting with what you should do.

DOS

As a teen, when it comes to dating, **do**:

⊙ Find someone that you feel comfortable with. You should feel like you can be comfortable with your partner and that you can have different opinions without it being an issue. Trusting each other when you are separated is also a big sign that someone makes you feel comfortable. You also should date someone that you do not feel pressured around.

⊙ Make sure that you exist as your own person outside of the relationship. It can be really easy to get wrapped up in the relationship, which can make you lose who you are as a person. Make sure you have interests that are yours and yours alone, and make sure that you spend time without your partner around too.

⊙ Know that there is a difference between conflict that is good and conflict that is bad because they're not the same thing. Conflict can make your relationship stronger if you avoid generalizing, do not bring up the past, say things that are productive, and explain how you feel while allowing your partner to do the same.

⊙ Understand the signs of an abusive relationship because it can happen to anyone—even boys. Some signs of an abusive relationship include:

⊙ Being overly critical of you.

⊙ Trying to isolate you from friends and family.

- Demanding to check your phone or other private items.

- Using social media to keep tabs on you at all times.

- Threatening you if you want to break up.

- Forcing you to do things that you do not want to do.

- Hurting you, either physically or emotionally.

DON'TS

In addition, it is important that while dating as a teen, you don't:

- Forget your friends. It is really common for people to enter into relationships and then drop all of their friends. Don't let this happen. Not only is it unfair to your friends, but you won't have a support system when and if you need it.

- Hide from problems in the relationship.

HOW TO ASK SOMEONE OUT

Entering into a relationship can be the scariest part—how do you ask someone out? For starters, do not overthink the situation. It is not that serious, and the worst thing that they can do is say no, which we'll talk about too. Don't let yourself ruminate on asking someone you like out. Just form a plan and go for it!

It is also a good idea to express your emotions as you ask your prospective partner out. Be straight up with them, telling them how you feel and why you feel that way. Be honest and be yourself, and it should be fine. If you do not know how to start the conversation, small talk is always the way to go!

SAMPLE SCRIPT FOR ASKING SOMEONE OUT

You may not know what to say, so here's an example of what you might say.

- You: Hey! I was really wanting to go see this movie, but I haven't been able to yet. Have you seen it?

- Them: No, but I wanted to see it too! It seemed really interesting and it is based on my favorite book.

- You: Oh, that's awesome! I didn't know it was based on a book. I'll have to check it out sometime!

- **Them:** For sure! It is a really interesting read and I couldn't put it down. I'd love to go see it in the theater.

- **You:** Oh, I have an idea. I think it is showing at the plaza this weekend. Would you maybe want to go see it together?

- **Them:** That sounds great! It is a plan.

HANDLING REJECTION

Sometimes, people are going to turn you down, and that's a normal part of dating. If you do get rejected, accept that the other person may not feel the same way about you that you feel about them. Respond positively, and recognize that their rejection isn't a reflection on you as a person.

CONSENT

Consent is the most important part of dating as a teen—and that's not an opinion; it is a fact. Consent cannot be avoided, nor should it be. Consent is, in short, the permission necessary for something to happen. This is a term that's usually used in the context of sex, but consent can and should also exist when it comes to things like hugging and hand-holding as well.

Anything that involves you touching someone else is something that warrants consent. The reason that consent is so important is because physical boundaries are fluid. What we enjoy one day may differ, and we may be uncomfortable with certain things at certain times. Negating consent is one of the worst things a person can do. It is traumatizing, immoral, and can ruin the lives of all parties involved.

Not only is it important to respect the consent of others, but it is important to make sure others respect your consent too. There are a few different elements of consent to be aware of ("Consent," 2016):

- Consent must be mutual. All parties involved must agree to whatever is happening in order for it to be consensual.

- Consent must be continuous. Consent doesn't end as soon as someone says "yes." You have to check up on them to make sure that consent has not been revoked—as is the right of someone to do so.

- Consent must be asked for each time, every time. Just because someone consents to something once does not mean they've consented to it forever.

- Consent must be able to be stopped. Someone can change their mind at any time.

- Consent must be verbally communicated. Silence or a lack of opposition is not consent.

In addition, you need to know that consent extends beyond just saying "no." In fact, if someone hasn't given an enthusiastic "yes," then consent hasn't been received. Furthermore, it is important to note that someone who is intoxicated, scared, or otherwise not in their right mind cannot consent. Situations that require consent include anything physical in nature, as well as anything that may make a person vulnerable.

SOCIAL MEDIA

Lastly, we're going to discuss social media, which is one of the places you probably spend most of your time. There are two important aspects of social media that we need to discuss: safety and etiquette.

ONLINE SAFETY

Being safe online might not be a big concern of yours, but take it from someone who has been on social media for a while; you never regret being too safe online. A lot of times, you can only recognize the true value of internet safety once you've been in an unsafe situation. It is better to be safe than sorry.

In general, it is easy to stay safe on social media if you follow the following advice:

- If you think something has happened that is unsafe, do not hesitate to voice your concerns to a parent or other trusted adult.

- Even if someone is saying something online that you disagree with, be respectful. Sometimes, people react harshly to being criticized online. It is best to stay safe by remaining respectful.

- Understand that you deserve privacy and respect the privacy of others too. You can change your privacy settings to control who is and is not allowed to see your information.

- Making new friends is great and online friends can sometimes become the best of friends. But before you accept a person into your circle, look at their profile and see what you have in common, like mutual friends, a school, or a hometown. You shouldn't accept friend requests from random people with no motivation to contact you. Remember that online, you can be anyone, and some people use that power for evil.

⊙ Be wary of job offers online, especially if you didn't recently apply to anything.

⊙ Trust your gut if something feels sketchy.

Keeping yourself safe online is the best way to avoid a potential nightmare online. I also recommend keeping your last name off the internet, as well as avoiding posting any photos of your family. Don't post anything of yourself that you wouldn't let your parents see, either.

SOCIAL MEDIA ETIQUETTE

There are also a handful of rules you should follow on social media. Of course, there isn't really anyone to regulate the internet; we have no "internet police," so to speak. Because of that, it is important to try and maintain a safe and respectful atmosphere online, which means everyone has to play their part. Here are some internet etiquette tips that you may find useful as you surf the web:

⊙ Make sure that you behave toward others in the same way you hope they'd respond to you. Don't say anything online to someone if you wouldn't say it to them in real life too.

⊙ Remember your digital footprint. Everywhere you go online, there is some trace of what you post that ties it back to you—even if you delete whatever it is. It is best not to post anything you'd regret later on.

⊙ A lot of people engage in sexting, which involves sharing sexually explicit messages online. I implore you to avoid doing this. Not only is it a federal crime to send or receive sexting images or videos, but there has been an increase in virtual sexual predators who will hack or manipulate you into your private business. Avoid posting or sharing anything sexually explicit online.

⊙ Don't post anything while you are angry. This can lead to you saying something that you do not mean online.

⊙ Remember that your words do affect others and that a mean word online can do just as much damage as a mean word in real life.

- Be careful with personal information like names, addresses, passwords, locations, etc.

By keeping in mind internet etiquette as you browse the web, you keep yourself and others safe.

CONVERSATION STARTERS!

If you are strapped for conversation starters, use some of these to guide you along:

1. What do you like to do on the weekends?

2. If you could have any superpower, what would it be and why?

3. What is the most interesting animal you've ever seen or learned about?

4. If you could travel anywhere in the world, where would you go, and what would you do there?

5. What is your favorite piece of media? Can you tell me why you like it?

6. If you could invent a new toy, what would it be, and how would it work?

7. What's the funniest thing you've ever experienced?

8. If you could be any fictional character for just one day, who would you be, and what would you do with your day?

9. What is your favorite outdoor activity or game to play with friends?

10. If you could have a magical pet, what kind of animal would it be, and what magical abilities would it have?

In this chapter, you learned everything that you need to know about relationships, dating, friendships, and being a teen online. Now, let's move on to focusing on landing you the first job of your dreams.

YOUR IDEAL MATE

Dating is hard - and sometimes we get lost in whether or not a potential mate will like us or not. But what if we don't like them? It's just as important to know what we sort of qualities we are looking for in someone we are dating. Here's a chance to make a list of the qualities we seek. But keep in mind that not every single quality needs to be present. Remember - no one's perfect.

Chapter 5: Landing Your Dream Job

You're encroaching upon the age at which you have to start getting your first job or two and preparing for a lifelong career. How exciting! This chapter is going to teach you everything you need to know about securing first jobs or fifth jobs, preparing you for a lifetime of success in your career endeavors.

FIGURING OUT THE WORK THAT WORKS FOR YOU

Do you know what you want to be when you "grow up"? Are you sure of a profession right now? I'm willing to bet that you are not, and that's perfectly okay—most teens do not know what they want to do for the rest of their lives. The work you do now in figuring out the work that works for you sets the stage for your future.

SELF ASSESSMENTS

It is important to find the right career for you so that you can begin preparing for it early on. One of the easiest ways to find some direction when it comes to picking out a career is to take a career self-assessment test, many of which can be found for free online. Actually, your school might also have career services that you can ask a counselor or librarian about as well. But anyway, taking a career exam will help you evaluate what you enjoy, what you are good at, and what's important to you in order to present you with the most ideal career options for you at this time. This is especially helpful if you have absolutely no idea what you might want to do.

CONSIDER YOUR STRENGTHS

You should also look up careers that are aligned with your strengths as a person—both academically and otherwise. Make a list of things you feel like you excel at, and try to find career opportunities that are in line with this. A career that is in tune with what you are naturally good at doing in every sense of the word is going to be best because it will allow you opportunities to build confidence while also challenging yourself to continuously do better.

CHECK OUT JOB DESCRIPTIONS

If you find a career or field that seems interesting, look at current job listings and see what some of the requirements are. Usually, jobs will list both hard and soft skills. Hard skills are ones like having a relevant degree, for example. Soft skills are going to be things like time management, confidence, and problem-solving skills. Having a good mix of hard and soft skills will allow you to be the prime candidate for a position. See what hard and soft skills, degrees, and other requirements are typical for a job in your desired field. This will help you set goals accordingly.

SELF REFLECT

Taking a bit of time to reflect on yourself is a good way to dive into finding out a career that will work for you. Consider what you are good at and what you enjoy, and even what types of things have led to failure in the past. Think about what your ideal work environment is and why, as well as your long-term goals and what you need to get to where you want to be with your career. By answering these questions, you will be able to think about what jobs are in line with your values and needs. You should also re-evaluate often to see if your career values have changed over time.

FINDING A MENTOR

People get mentors for a lot of reasons. Sometimes people get mentors to help them reach personal goals, while others get mentors to help them accomplish something specific in terms of life. You may opt to find a mentor who can directly help you with your career decisions, which is a great choice if you are someone who benefits heavily from one-on-one guidance. You can find mentors online, through bulletin boards, and more.

LIST OUT OPTIONS

Think about every possible job you might like to do, and write it down. For each job, list out the pros and cons of that job, including things like salary, job requirements, experience levels, and more. This presents you with a visual for what jobs might be a better match than others and how you can accomplish each possible option. Plus, this helps you if you think your options are limited in nature. For example, you might think that there is nothing you can do with your current skills, but once you get to listing things out, you may find a dozen or more career options available to you.

NETWORK AND GAIN EXPERIENCE

Internships are perfect for networking and gaining experience. Even volunteering can help you out significantly. Networking is a beneficial way to build up your career prospects and opportunities by connecting with others both in and outside of the field you are considering going into. Internships and volunteering opportunities are able to provide you with tangible work experiences that allow you to build up your resume—something we'll talk about working on soon. I strongly recommend finding a volunteer or internship opportunity—even if it is online—if you do not have enough extracurriculars as is in order to amplify career possibilities.

DO WHAT MAKES YOU HAPPY

My last piece of advice for finding a job that works for you is to do what makes you happy, even if you are not sure that it can help you when it comes to your potential career options. Doing what makes you happy can open far more doors than you may expect, granting you opportunities to experience a life of what you love.

HOW TO WRITE YOUR FIRST RESUME

Writing a strong resume is going to be one of the best things you will do for yourself when it comes to finding a career and other opportunities in life. A resume is essentially a sheet of paper that condenses all of your major skills and attributes so that potential employers and others interested in hiring you for something can take a look at it. Unfortunately, there are a lot of wrong ways to write up a resume, so it is important that you make a good first impression with your own.

THE RESUME WRITING PROCESS

Writing a resume may look a little bit different for everyone, but for you, I recommend following these steps:

1. Gather your personal information. The personal information that you will need for your resume includes your name, city, phone number, email address, any work experience you have, academic experience, extracurriculars, and anything else you may have.

2. Pick a resume layout. I recommend using a Google Docs template or another free template online to design your resume. Find one that you feel is indicative of your personality while still remaining professional.

3. Fill out your personal information and contact information first. If someone is interested in you based on your resume, then they'll need a way to reach out, either by phone or email. Preferably, you should include both, but you do not need to add your full address.

4. Include a summary or objective at the top of your resume, such as a statement of intent. This can look something like "[Name] is a hardworking high school student looking for their first job. They excel in [list your strengths]."

5. List your work experience, education, and any achievements or awards you've won.

6. Mention your hard and soft skills, as I talked about earlier.

7. Include any additional languages you know, hobbies you have, and projects you engage with.

8. Craft a cover letter to go with your resume, wherein you introduce yourself, talk about why you want the job, and why you are qualified.

9. Proofread both your resume and cover letter.

This will help you build the perfect resume!

OTHER RESUME TIPS

Before I send you off to write your very own resume, I have a handful of additional tips to guide you to success. For example, you are going to want to look at a prospective job listing that you are applying for. Check out some of the keywords in the listing, and align your resume with those keywords. It is also a good idea to look at samples of other resumes for people who've applied to similar jobs and see how you can fine-tune your resume based on those ones.

Additionally, it is important to maintain a high degree of professionalism in your resume. Don't use fancy fonts or colors. Your resume should be mostly in black and white, with maybe one color for headings or to set apart certain aspects of your layout. Use a serif font or another basic font that's easily readable so that prospective employers can easily read your resume. While lots of colors and fun fonts may look cool, a professional-looking resume shows that you know how to be professional when the time calls for it. You should also omit any irrelevant information for the same reason.

Furthermore, you might not have work experience and you will need to put something on your resume. Don't worry if you are searching for your first job. Instead of work experience, there are a few alternatives you have. For instance, you can emphasize your education as a primary part of your resume, highlighting your grades, test scores, and extracurriculars. If you are looking for a job with any academic context, think about how you can play your education to your benefit. Also, instead of work experience, you can add internships and volunteering as a highlight of your resume. It is possible to land a great job without work experience so long as you have a stellar resume and cover letter otherwise.

HOW TO GIVE A MEMORABLE ELEVATOR PITCH

A lot of people do not use elevator pitches anymore, but they're actually still very effective; it is just that most people do not take the time to develop one! An elevator pitch is a short and persuasive pitch that you give to someone to introduce yourself and what you have to offer. It is meant to inspire someone to feel interested in who you are and what you've got going for you. An elevator pitch is meant to be brief, maybe 30 seconds at most—just enough time to provide on an elevator.

An elevator pitch is going to consist of a few key things:

1. Introduce yourself. Keep it short and simple, ideally limiting it to your name and a courtesy phrase. For example, you might use something like, "Hi, my name is Brad and it is wonderful to meet you."

2. From there, you are going to explain what you do. Right now, since you are a student, your elevator pitch is probably going to consist of some of

your major achievements and accomplishments. For example, you might say something like, "I'm the president of my school's robotics team, where I oversee the successful completion of projects, test new designs and code, and work toward a common goal of [insert goal of current project]." This is a good second step in your pitch because it tells them what your title is and what you do—things that make you stand out from other people.

3. Then, you are going to tell whoever you are talking to what you want from them. Why are you giving them this pitch? Something you might say could be, "I'm heavily interested in your robotics department's internship opportunity, as it seems to be important work with a strong direction. I would love the opportunity to use what I know to contribute to your mission." This is a good third step because it conveys what you want, why you are interested, and implies how this could benefit the person that you are speaking to.

4. Finally, you are going to give a call to action, something that inspires the person you are speaking to to make a decision or forward motion. For example, you could ask, "Would it be alright for us to schedule a time to talk about this opportunity together next week?" This is both assertive and shows initiative, indicating that you are rearing for the position and have what it takes.

If you follow these steps, you are sure to convey a convincing elevator pitch that takes you to great places. Be sure to avoid rambling and practice your elevator pitch to yourself before using it in person!

HOW TO ACE YOUR JOB INTERVIEW

So you've got an interview. Congratulations are in order! Getting an interview is an amazing first step when it comes to landing your first job. But once you've got the interview, how do you then secure the job? That's what we're going to talk about now.

HOW TO PREPARE FOR AN INTERVIEW

Preparing for an interview can seem daunting, especially if it is your first one. But personally, I've gone through more interviews than I can count over the years, and I have a few steps that will help you get ready to ace any interview that you embark upon. The steps are:

1. Look at the job posting for the job that you are interviewing for. As you get ready for your interview, use the job description to guide you. It is going to list qualifications and what the employer is looking for in their perfect employee. By taking a look at this description, you can work to align yourself more closely with what they deem to be ideal, giving yourself a better shot at success. Plus, job descriptions can often key you into things the interviewer may ask.

2. Think about why you are qualified for the job, and be prepared to explain why you are the best person for the role. Even if you seem like the ideal candidate on paper, they're going to want to know that you have the confidence to put yourself out there when it comes to an interview.

3. Research the company and the role you are applying for, learning about the company's history and values. This will give you an advantage when it comes to making yourself seem like an ideal candidate.

4. Think about common answers to interview questions—something we'll dive into more depth in the next chapter.

5. Practice talking to an interviewer at home by giving yourself a fake interview and working on confidence in your voice and body language as you do. This will help ensure that you are going to do an excellent job at the real thing.

6. Plan some thoughtful questions to ask your interviewer about their job, themselves, or their role to show interest. Prospective employers use these questions to learn more about you and your values as well.

7. Print out a physical copy of your resume. While your interviewer may have your resume printed out on their own, it looks very impressive if you come with a hard copy for them to reference.

8. After the interview, you have to follow up. Either send an email or make a phone call thanking the interviewer for their time, connect the interview to your passions, and welcome them to ask any questions. Finish off with an "I'm looking forward to your decision" and you are good to go!

QUESTIONS THEY MAY ASK AND WHAT TO ANSWER

In addition, it is good to be prepared for some of the questions they may ask you because a lot of interviewers do ask questions! Fortunately, there are some very common questions you may be asked. While your answers are going to vary because everyone is different, I've provided you with some common questions and good answers to them that you can tweak for your own interview.

1. Q: Why are you looking for a job?
   A: I'm looking for a job because I want more experience within the industry. It is something I'm passionate about, and I would love more hands-on experience while I have the spare time. Additionally, it is financially responsible because I'm currently saving for college, as that will be a big step forward in achieving my goals.

2. Q: Why do you want to work for us?
   A: I would like to work for this company because I feel like the company's values align closely with my own. I'm fond of joining a team that has values in line with my own, and the work environment seems amazing here. In the future, I hope to accomplish [goal], and this job would be a wonderful opportunity to get the kind of experience that I'm looking for.

3. Q: Why are you the best candidate for the position?
   A: I'm the best person for the job due to my dedication and work ethic. I love being a proactive coworker in a fast-paced environment, and I've always believed that working hard is the key to doing well in life. I'm a reliable person who can work both quickly and effectively as well.

4. Q: What is one of your biggest accomplishments?
   A: Be honest and talk earnestly about one of your most important accomplishments and why it is so important to you.

5. Q: Where do you see yourself five years from now?
   A: The only wrong answer to this question is "I do not know." Come prepared with something to say about your future academic and professional goals, and feel free to be honest—so long as you have some idea of the direction you want to shoot for.

6. Q: What is a problem you've had recently and how did you solve it?
   A: This question is aimed at determining if you are able to solve problems quickly and rationally. Make up and rehearse a story that highlights a problem you've solved and how you solved it, exhibiting time management and critical thinking skills in the process.

If you walk into the interview prepared to answer these questions, then you are already off to a wonderful start when it comes to acing your interview. All that's left is actually answering them!

PROFESSIONAL ETIQUETTE

Understanding professional etiquette is a big part of your first job. You're going to need to be able to navigate various situations with an element of professionalism and dignity, but these things do not always come naturally for many people—especially when you are a teen working your first job. Let's briefly explore some rules of etiquette you will need to know for work.

WORKPLACE ETIQUETTE

Each place you work at throughout the course of your life is going to have different rules and expectations regarding how you act. But there are, however, a few things that are universal to each job:

- Respect the schedule that your employer provides. If you've never heard the saying "early is on time and on time is late," now's the time to get acquainted with it. You should show up at least five minutes before you are scheduled to work, and you can't leave without permission. If you need to call in sick or for another reason, you should do so as early in advance as you can and try to help find someone to cover your shift. In addition, it is a courtesy to give your boss two weeks' notice before you stop working for them.

- Be ready to look good and professional. You should dress in clean clothes that have no wrinkles, logos, or phrases on them, and you should make sure that your body is clean and smells good as well. If you work with food or retail, avoid having overgrown nails, and do not wear nail polish in food service. A good rule is to dress for the job you want, not the job you have.

- Stay off of your phone at work. You do not need your phone during work unless your employer specifically requires it, and if there is some emergency wherein you need your phone, let your boss know ahead of time. Otherwise, consider work to be a screen-free area.

- Don't drag personal problems into the workplace. If you have a personal issue that your boss needs to be aware of, talk to them privately before your shift begins.

⊙ Learn from your mistakes and take accountability.

EMAIL ETIQUETTE

There are also certain etiquette rules that you should follow when it comes to sending emails—rules that will make you more professional and allow you to communicate effectively:

⊙ Every email should have a greeting and a closing. Start the email with something friendly and end by signing off your name and including your contact information.

⊙ Your subject line should be concise and clear, indicating what the email is about before your email is even opened.

⊙ Be kind in your tone and avoid all capitals, excess punctuation, etc. Avoid using text speak.

Now you know everything you need in order to land your perfect job, ace those interviews, and succeed at work. Let's keep moving forward to discuss something else that you might be struggling with as a teen—finances.

PREPARE YOUR PITCH

An elevator pitch is a short and persuasive pitch that you give to someone to introduce yourself and what you have to offer. Use this space to create your own elevator pitch so that you're prepared when the opportunity arises.

Chapter 6: Exercising Financial Fitness

Let's face it: you are not going to be wealthy as a teen… at least, not unless your family is incredibly financially fortunate. Managing expenses as a teenager is the first look that you get into managing expenses as an adult, and it can honestly be very confusing. Finances are one of the most perplexing things that many teens deal with, which is why it is so important to learn financial fitness early on. By the end of this chapter, you will understand key components of financial fitness that allow you to manage your money effectively—including budgeting tips, what a credit card is, and smart money habits you will need to know.

THE BASICS OF BUDGETING

Understanding the in's and out's of budgeting is probably the most important first step in succeeding financially. Don't worry; I've got your back—we'll tackle this together.

WHAT IS A BUDGET?

You have to know a thing before you can use it; budgeting is no different. A budget can be defined as a plan for spending habits based on money that moves in and money that flows out. One's budget serves as a rough estimate of how much money you are going to spend each day, week, month, or even year. Some people budget their everyday expenses, while others opt to keep a more broad monthly budget. Regardless of the scope of your particular budget, it is important that you have one at the minimum.

WHY IS BUDGETING IMPORTANT?

Just what makes budgeting so important? There are actually dozens of reasons why budgeting is so important, but we'll stick to a few of the main ones for now. Budgeting is important because it helps you avoid spending money that you do not have. In other words, having a solid budget will allow you to allocate money flawlessly, avoiding a situation where you've spent money you needed elsewhere. Budgeting also helps you meet various financial goals, including being able to retire happily. Furthermore, budgeting prepares you in the case of an emergency situation, ensuring that you are always financially secure no matter what life throws at you. As it stands, there is no downside to budgeting, which means that there is no excuse to avoid developing one.

BUDGETING STRATEGIES

So now that you know what a budget is and why it is important, it is time to explore how you can effectively budget yourself. The following are five different budgeting strategies that you can apply to your own finances in order to experience severe success when it comes to budgeting your money (Jordan, 2019):

1. The zero-based budget. This budget refers to a plan where your income matches your outcome, meaning that the money coming into your account is equal to the money you spend. However, this doesn't mean that you are spending all of your money in a traditional sense; rather, the zero-based budgeting technique includes savings and investing as spending because you are paying the account. Zero-based budgeting sounds like a no-brainer, but for many people, it is actually a struggle. Some people have positive bank accounts where every dollar is not accounted for, while others have negative accounts from overspending. Both can be avoided with this tactic.

2. The pay-yourself-first budget. This budgeting option involves paying your future self before you spend any of your money. So instead of spending your money on the newest game, first, you have to deposit money into your savings account. This may also seem like an obvious method, but a lot of people overlook just how effective it can be!

3. The envelope budget system. This is essentially the zero-based budget with cash. It can be easy to spend money unwisely when it is all digital because our brains do not often register that what we're spending is money. When you use cash, you can fill each envelope you've labeled for each aspect of your budget and physically see where money needs to be allocated.

4. The 50/30/20 budget. Under this budgeting method, you break your expenses down based on percentages. 50% of your money should go toward necessary expenses, 30% toward whatever you decide, and 20% directly to savings.

5. The "no" budget. This involves paying attention to how much money you have, understanding when bills hit your account, saving for emergency expenses, and then spending what's left over without withdrawing your account. This is a method of budgeting without "budgeting," if you know what I mean.

HOW TO GROW YOUR MONEY

Lastly, let's talk about growing your money—because everyone loves extra money. There are plenty of things that you can do in order to help your money grow.

KNOW YOUR INCOME

Understanding how much money you bring in is important. You might make $15 an hour, but what do you make per check after taxes? It is important to understand this because your hourly wage and your take-home pay are different. If you budget for your hourly and not your take-home pay, there are going to be gaps that you cannot fill within your budget.

CREATE BUDGET CATEGORIES

Make sure you have everything you need before starting the laundry. Scan for spills and pre-treat any that you detect. Spot treatments are effective for many stains, while more intensive procedures are necessary for others.

Make sure you have plenty of toilet paper and tissues on hand to prevent any mishaps. To prevent snagging, remove belts and jewelry, take out coins, and fasten buttons and zippers.

PICK A BUDGETING STRATEGY

Don't just read about them. Go back to the budgeting strategies that I gave you and select one you want to follow or research a different one that you feel works better for you. Try to refrain from allowing your budget to fall for chance, and use your budgeting strategy every time you get paid for the best results.

SAVE FIRST, SPEND LATER

Don't just read about them. Go back to the budgeting strategies that I gave you and select one you want to follow or research a different one that you feel works better for you. Try to refrain from allowing your budget to fall for chance, and use your budgeting strategy every time you get paid for the best results.

SET GOALS

Set financial goals for yourself and stick to them, even if it means adjusting your budgeting a little bit in order to meet those goals. Track your spending habits over time and see where you have room to change things up a bit.

START YOUR OWN SAVINGS ACCOUNT

As you can probably tell based on the last section, an important part of being financially smart is opening your own savings account and actually using it. Understanding the process for opening a bank account, the requirements for having the account, and potential features to look out for can ensure that you select the right savings account for you.

THE PROCESS

When you go to the bank in order to open a savings account, your parent is probably going to need to be there to help you. This is because minors cannot open a bank account on their own due to age restrictions, which means that your parents have to do it for you or be present for you to do it yourself. When you go, there are a few things you will probably benefit from having with you:

- your parent's ID
- your own ID if you have one
- your birth certificate and social security card
- proof of address other than your ID
- bank account information if you already have a bank account
- contact information, like your phone number and an email address

In some cases, all of this may not be needed, but it is going to be best if you go to the bank with everything you *might* need just in case.

When you go, your parents can set the account up for you. Although, I recommend taking the initiative and talking to the banker yourself. When you arrive, you can tell them something like "Hi! My name is [Name]. I'm [age], and I want to set up my first savings account. My parents are here to help me." With that, the banker will be able to guide you in the right direction.

Usually, the banker will take you to an office or seat and ask you a few questions about yourself. This is standard information, and they will fill out your profile in their system. Generally, the banker may ask you to set a password in case you need to request information over the phone. Remember this password! After a few more questions, the banker will give you your account information and you can begin depositing.

FEATURES TO LOOK OUT FOR

Different banks are going to offer different features associated with their savings accounts. It might be tempting to allow your parents to take you to whatever bank they go to, but you should take the time to do your research into the pros and cons of various banks and find one with savings account features that will help you meet your goals. Some of the features savings accounts can offer include:

- No minimum deposit. Some banking and savings accounts are going to make you have a minimum amount deposited in them at first, which can be challenging if you are just starting out your savings account. Fortunately, a lot of savings accounts come with an option for no minimum deposit, which I heavily recommend looking into unless you have a lot of cash lying around to deposit.

- No monthly fees. While most banks will charge a small fee just to keep your account open with them, there are plenty of banks that do not charge you anything at all. Try to find a bank that doesn't charge monthly fees for having a savings account—the few dollars can really add up over time!

- Online banking. Banks are increasingly offering mobile and online banking features in order to revolutionize and modernize banking. But you can't assume that every bank offers this, nor that every bank offers this for free. Before committing to an institution, check out what options they have regarding online banking. This can allow you to add money to your savings account and monitor its balance from the comfort of your own home.

- Instant deposits and transfers. Some banks offer the option where, each month or each week, you can elect to have some of your money automatically deducted from your checking account and deposited into savings. If you are a forgetful person, this can be an awesome way to keep up with adding to your savings account regularly.

Not every savings account is going to come with all features, but you may be able to find some compelling options. Be sure to research banking institutions in your area and do not fall for completely internet-based banks, as many of these can ruin your credit score and make your life more difficult in the future. And speaking of credit, that's what we'll talk about next.

BUILDING CREDIT

Credit scores are one of those boring adult things that sneak up on you—they do not matter until suddenly they do. Credit scores do not have to be hard or confusing, though; let's talk about what credit scores are!

WHAT IS A CREDIT SCORE

Credit scores are three-digit numbers that range from around 300 to 850. It shows people who you may ask for a loan in the future how reliable you are in repaying those loans. In other words, your credit score shows how reliable you are with following through on repayments. This means that you can continue to borrow more money moving forward. The three major bureaus are Equifax, Experian, and Transunion, and it is possible to have a slightly different score with each bureau.

WHAT FACTORS IMPACT YOUR CREDIT SCORE?

Your credit score is impacted by a lot of things, and it is important to understand what impacts it because some things won't make sense at first. Primarily, your credit is impacted by your payment history (whether you pay loans and credit cards back on time), how much debt you owe, how long your credit history is, how many types of credit you have, and how many times you've applied for credit cards, loans, etc. Each of these things impacts your score differently, with the first things I listed having more of an impact. As such, it is really important to make sure to keep up with debt repayments and your credit cards when you eventually open them.

WHY DOES YOUR CREDIT MATTER?

You might be thinking that your credit score is irrelevant. After all, if you ignore it, then it has no impact on your life, right? Well, no. Many different areas of your life are impacted by having a good credit score; people with high credit scores experience a lot of financial benefits as well. If you have a high credit score, then you may be able to receive better interest rates on things like credit cards, car payments, and various other loans later in life. In addition, a low credit score is all a prospective landlord needs in order to turn you down for an apartment. Higher credit scores also make utilities cheaper as well.

HOW TO BUILD CREDIT

The best way to build your credit is to apply for a credit card. You can build your credit as a minor by becoming authorized on someone else's card or having your parents open one for you. Remember that credit cards aren't "free money," as most people think. If you do not pay the money back, then your credit score will take a major hit. The best thing to do is open a credit card, make regular small purchases on it, and then pay them off immediately.

MAINTAINING A GOOD CREDIT SCORE

You can maintain a good credit score easily. It is not like credit bureaus hide the secrets of a good credit score from you. People have bad credit due to irresponsible decisions made for various reasons, and you should avoid letting that be you. Don't make any late payments on your credit cards, keep your credit balance low, and only keep one credit card at first. Pay your bills on time, and you should be fine.

SMART MONEY HABITS

Knowing all of this, you might be wondering what else you can do to amplify your successes when it comes to finances. As it turns out, there are a ton of things that you can do to minimize spending, maximize savings, and have a good life in the meantime.

KEEP TRACK OF EXPENSES

It is always important to keep track of your expenses. Everything you spend money on should be recorded, no matter how small. For example, even if you only buy a two-dollar drink, write it down. You might find that over time, you buy a lot of two-dollar drinks that ultimately accumulate to be ineffective cost-wise. Plus, if you do not track your finances responsibly, it can be easy to lose track of large sums of money in the blink of an eye. Because of this, it is the responsible and financially intelligent thing to do to keep track of every cent that comes into or out of your account. You'll never have unaccounted-for money if you do this.

LEARN FROM MISTAKES

Everybody makes mistakes; it is just a fact of life. You're going to make financial mistakes as you progress through your teenage years. Just remember that the best thing you can do is learn from these mistakes. For example, if you have to deal with an overdraft fee because you overdraft your account to buy a video game, then learn from your mistake and avoid overdrafting again in the future—overdraft fees often cost us more money than they're worth. When you make a financial mistake, make sure that you are aware of the repercussions and be responsible for them, and avoid making similar mistakes in the future.

EARN MORE WITH A SIDE HUSTLE

Side hustles are an awesome way to earn extra cash. You know how in older shows and movies, people mowed lawns for extra money? That's still something that you can do! You can offer to mow people's lawns or clean up their spaces, pet or babysit, or even do things online in order to earn some extra money in your spare time. If you work a job and have a side hustle, not only do you earn extra money, but you work on finding passions and things that you can potentially do for a career as well.

SPEND MINIMALLY

It is going to suck, but you can make a really smart decision if you opt to spend minimally while you are in high school. This is because you probably have a lot of things that you want to buy, but having savings in the future is going to be so vital to ensuring your happiness.

AVOID PEER PRESSURE AND FOMO

Going out with friends is a fun part of growing up, but sometimes we unintentionally spend more than we had to spend when we go out with friends. Buying food, drinks, clothes, movie tickets, and other items while out with friends can be fun, but if you've not allocated money for this, you are just dipping into your savings. While with your friends, be honest and let them know that you are saving and won't be able to spare money on an impromptu video game splurge, for instance. You should also try your best to avoid the fear of missing out, also known as FOMO. FOMO can cause us to do the same thing—spending money we didn't mean to—just so we do not feel like we missed out on an experience. It'll be hard, but working through FOMO is more rewarding in the end than anything you'd have done in the moment.

ASK FOR HELP

If you need help from someone with more financial wisdom than you, do not be afraid to ask. Even if you've found yourself in a bit of a bad situation financially, it is better not to have to walk through the struggle alone. Your parents might be mad if you've done something extreme financially, but at the end of the day, they'll be able to help you minimize the damages and improve your chances of success moving forward.

HAVE FUN WITHOUT SPENDING

There are so many things you can do without spending money. I know it is tempting to go out with friends, but if you really want to save money and do not have anything to spend while going out, try suggesting something like a sleepover. It might seem juvenile, but try suggesting it! You might be surprised by how many of your friends would love to just chill indoors, play a game together, and maybe pool money for a pizza in order to enjoy an evening without spending too much money at all. Not everyone has ample finances to spend on going out with friends, and by making this suggestion, you are helping yourself out as well as any friends you have who may not want to speak up.

BE FINANCIALLY WISE ABOUT COLLEGE

I know how boring those meetings about student loans, scholarships, and whatnot can be as you prepare to apply for college. They seem to drone on and are stressful. But I want to really encourage you to pay attention, not just to financial options, but to how you can best use your finances as you navigate college applications. A lot of people end up thousands, if not hundreds of thousands of dollars in debt because they didn't listen to sound advice when it comes to college apps. Don't be one of those people!

TAKE ADVANTAGE OF YOUR STUDENT ID

I do not know if you know this, but if you have a student ID, ask around about student discounts when you go to the store or go out to eat. A lot of places, especially chain restaurants, offer really good deals for students if you can show them a current student ID. This is a smart, free, and easy way to save a few dollars every single time you leave the house, allowing you to spend that money on something else.

To sum it up, one of the smartest things you will do as a teen is taking the initiative to learn financial literacy. With the skills I've presented to you throughout this chapter, you will be able to handle any financial difficulty like a boss—and make it look easy too!

TIME TO BUDGET

It's time to put what you've learned to the test. Using this worksheet, create your own budget based on possible future income and expenses. This will help you prepare for a future career, lifestyle, and even where you plan to settle down.

RENT _____

GROCERIES _____

NATURAL GAS _____

ELECTRICITY _____

WATER & SEWER _____

GAS _____

PHONE _____

CAR INSURANCE _____

MEDICAL INSURANCE _____

ENTERTAINMENT _____

CLOTHING _____

Chapter 7: Caring for Your First Car

Getting your first car is one of the most exciting things that can happen to you as a teen. I remember when I got my first car—how happy I was and excited for the new opportunities that opened up. If you have or are soon to get your very first car, you might be feeling the same way. Not to bog down your enthusiasm, but getting that car does come with its own unique set of responsibilities that have to be addressed.

Taking care of your car is vital. You need to know how to perform basic maintenance on your car, as well as other tips for driving, in order to be a good car owner. Trust me; it is easier to learn all this now and avoid having to pay thousands of dollars down the line when something serious goes wrong with your car. Whenever your first set of keys lands in your hand, you want to be prepared; that preparation begins right now!

CARING FOR YOUR CAR

Taking care of your car yourself is smart—it saves you money on repairs and can prevent a bad situation from occurring if you know basic car upkeep. Of course, certain things require a professional to take a look, but why not learn what you can to care for your car on your own? It'll show your parents that you are responsible enough to have the car, and it looks very impressive to know your way around a car!

CHECKING TIRE PRESSURE

Checking tire pressure is important because in order for your car to drive safely, the tire pressure has to be just right. There are a few times that you will want to be sure to check the pressure of all four of your car's tires. Once a month, after tire replacements, after running over something sharp, and after hitting a curb are all times that you should check your tire pressure. The perfect tire pressure for your car is going to be listed on a sticker somewhere in your car (usually the driver's side door). Checking tire pressure is easy because all you need is a tire pressure gauge. Check your tire pressure when your car is cooled down by removing the air valve cap, and then press the cause against the valve stem for about two seconds. Read the gauge and compare the number with what the pressure should be for your car. If it is perfect, replace the cap. Do this for all four tires.

Sometimes, your tires will need to be inflated or deflated. Inflate the tires by parking near the air pump, removing the valve caps, and pressing the nozzle to the valve stem. Remove the hose after a few seconds and check the tire pressure, repeating for each tire and then replacing the caps. To deflate the tires, you are going to press the black dot located on the back of your tire pressure gauge while it is attached to the valve stem and then check the tire pressure. Tada! Your tires are good to go!

CHANGING A TIRE

Don't get stuck in the middle of nowhere with a flat tire. Instead, follow these steps to change your car tire all by yourself ("How to Change a Flat Tire," 2021):

1. Pull over in a safe location. The ground should be solid and straight, and you should be in a well-lit area.

2. Turn on your hazard lights and the parking brake. This will keep you safe and let other drivers know to go around you carefully.

3. You're going to need a jack, a wrench, and a spare tire, but you might also like to have a flashlight, tire gauge, and the owner's manual for your car too. Keep all of this inside your car, just in case.

4. Now, you are going to loosen the lug nuts on your car. Pry off the hubcap first if your car has one, then use your wrench to loosen the lug nuts until each one can be turned by hand.

5. Use the jack to lift your car up. Place the jack under a metal part of your car; do not let the jack touch anything plastic, as this can cause it to break. Use the jack to raise the tire up, making sure that the jack stays on the ground.

6. Take the lug nuts off completely and keep them somewhere safe. Then pull your tire off the car.

7. Put the spare tire onto the car.

8. Replace the lug nuts, but only tighten them by hand.

9. Lower your car slowly until the tire starts to touch the ground, but do not let it go all the way. Then, tighten your lug nuts in the following order: 1, 3, 5, 2, 4.

10. Lower the car completely and finish tightening the lug nuts, and replace your hubcap if you have one.

Congrats! You changed your first tire.

WINDSHIELD WIPER FLUID

In order to check your windshield wiper fluid, open the hood of your car and secure it, then find the windshield wiper tube. It is probably going to be brightly colored—or at least the cap will be—and you will see a windshield image. Look at the side of the tube. Is the windshield wiper fluid at the fill line? If it is lower, you can add some fluid by pouring it into this tube until it reaches the fill line. Put the cap back on the tube, lower your hood, and you are done!

OIL CHECKS

Warm up your car first. The best time to check the oil is going to be when the car is warm. Park your car on a level surface and then locate the dipstick for the oil. It is going to be under the hood and most often has a circular handle that's yellow or orange. You're going to need a napkin, so grab one right quick. Then, carefully pull the dipstick out of its spot and wipe it off from handle to base. Once you've done that, place it back in the slot and wait for a second before removing it again. If your oil level is good, it'll be between the two circles or markers on the dipstick. If the oil level is low, so long as the texture is smooth, you can add more oil. But if it has a grainy texture, you need to go have your oil changed.

CHANGING HEADLIGHTS

Driving with busted headlights is illegal, and fixing it yourself is much cheaper than going to a shop to have it fixed. To change your headlight, first, turn the car off. Open the hood and find the headlight holder, which is going to be located at the front of the car. Then, disconnect the wires connecting the headlight and unscrew the old headlight. Screw the new headlight in, but be careful not to touch the glass part of it. Reconnect anything you disconnected and close your hood. You're good to go!

CHANGING WINDSHIELD WIPER BLADES

If your windshield wipers aren't working that well when you use them, then it is time to change them. The wipers will struggle to glide across the windshield as well, indicating that they should be changed. Buy windshield wipers that are specific to your car because each car is going to take something a little different. To replace the blades, take the new ones out of the packaging first. Then lift your existing windshield wiper and turn the blade at a perpendicular angle to the arm. There will be a little tab to flip to release the blade. Be very careful not to let the arm fall onto your windshield; if it does, it can crack the windshield. Remove the blade and then grab the new ones. Place it parallel to the arm and gently guide it into its slot, turn it perpendicular, and pull it a bit to lock it into place.

JUMPSTARTING A DEAD BATTERY

Practically nothing is worse than being stranded in the middle of nowhere with a dead car battery, which is why learning to jumpstart your car is crucial. You're going to need jumper cables and a working car or a jump box. Park the two cars close to one another and place them in park, turning the cars off completely and engaging the parking brake. Attach one of the cables to the positive side of the dead battery, then attach the other end to the positive side of the working battery. With the other cable, do the same things to the negative side, but start with the working car instead. Attach the last clip on the negative side to an unpainted piece of metal under the car's hood, ideally far from the battery. Start the working car and let it run for a few minutes before starting the dead car. If it comes on, detach the cables in the opposite order you applied them without turning your own car off. If it doesn't turn back on, give it a few more minutes, then try again.

DECIPHERING YOUR DASHBOARD

The dashboard of your car is the place with all of those confusing symbols behind the steering wheel. We're about to make those symbols a lot less confusing, allowing you to take better care of your car. Some of the most common dashboard lights that you will see include:

- Green or blue lights. These lights let you know that something is on or running in the car.

- Orange or yellow lights. These lights indicate that something needs to be repaired at some point in the near future.

- Red or flashing lights. These are lights that show your car is in urgent need of repair.

- Oil pressure warning. This light looks like a red oil can logo, and it indicates that your car is low on oil or that the oil pump isn't working correctly. Pull over and conduct an oil check if this is the case, and if filling the oil doesn't fix it, go to a mechanic immediately.

- Tire pressure warning. This light looks like an exclamation point in the middle of a parenthetical-looking symbol, which indicates that the pressure of your car tires is off. Check your car tire pressure as soon as possible.

- Engine temperature warning. This symbol looks like a thermometer bobbing in water, and it means that your engine is overheating. Turn off the air conditioner and turn on the heater to see if that helps. If not, pull over and let the engine cool, but do not open the hood. You will need to call a roadside service to help you out.

- Check engine light. This light looks like an engine and indicates that you need to get your engine checked by a professional.

- Battery alert. This is a red light that looks like a battery and means that something is wrong with your car's battery.

- Seat belt reminder. This light will look like a passenger with a seatbelt, and it'll remind you or whoever else is in your car to put on your seatbelt.

- Windshield fluid indicator. This light looks like a windshield with water and means that you need to top off your fluid.

STAYING SAFE ON THE ROAD

Even if you think you are a good driver, think about it this way: everyone else on the road thinks they're a good driver, yet every day, someone is killed in a car accident. To keep yourself safe, it is important to be aware of how you can drive in various conditions so that you do not get hurt while behind the wheel. Start the disabled vehicle after connecting the cords. Run both vehicles for three minutes after starting.

DEFENSIVE DRIVING

The best thing you can learn is defensive driving when it comes to tactics to keep yourself safe in the car. Some of the biggest defensive driving tips include ("The Keys to Defensive Driving," n.d.):

- Turn off your phone and put it out of sight. Distracted driving is never okay; it puts you and everyone on the road at risk.

- Avoid eating or drinking while driving, and keep any music turned down enough that you can hear horns and emergency vehicles.

- Leave enough space between you and the person in front of you.

- Don't change lanes at an intersection.

- Don't pass other drivers unless you've been given the go-ahead.

- Avoid using cruise control if it is wet or icy outside.

- Don't drive on an empty tank of gas.

- Keep an emergency kit in your car.

- Always know where you are.

- Don't get out of the car if it is on the road.

- Keep the doors locked and the windows rolled all the way up.

- Don't leave valuable items in plain sight.

DRIVING IN BAD WEATHER

Additionally, it is important to know how to drive in various bad weather conditions, even if you do not think it is something you will need. You never know when a sudden onset of bad weather can leave you stranded or get you into an accident.

DRIVING IN SNOW AND ICE

When it comes to snow and ice, you should always try to avoid driving whenever possible. But I know that sometimes you do have places to be, which is why it is important to follow these safe driving tips:

- Drive slowly; in the snow, your tires cannot grip the ground as well, making it necessary for you to drive slowly as well as accelerate and decelerate slowly.

- Drive with a greater distance between you and the car in front of you.

- Don't stop unless you absolutely have to, and do not power up or stop on hills.

DRIVING IN RAIN

Rain can decrease visibility and make the roads rather slick. If you are driving in the rain, some tips you can follow to keep you safe include:

- Driving in the rain is like driving in snow in that you have to drive slowly and leave room between you and the car in front of you.

- Use your low-light headlights.

- Pay attention to the potential for spray from bigger cars, as this can decrease your visibility.

DRIVING IN FOG

The last major bad weather situation you may have to drive in is the fog. Fog makes driving particularly hard because you can't see past a few feet in front of you. You can drive safely in the fog with these tips:

- Drive slowly and use your fog lights.

- Never use your high beams.

- Pay extra attention to the lines on the road.

OTHER SAFE DRIVING TIPS

To finish off this chapter, I want to elaborate upon some final safe driving tips that'll keep you safe when you are adventuring in your car. Keeping these safe driving tips in mind will help you avoid accidents and damages, as well as will allow you to do your part in keeping those around you safe.

MAKE PROPER ADJUSTMENTS BEFORE DRIVING

When you get into the car, there are going to be a number of adjustments that you need to make within the vehicle, especially if you share a car with a parent or sibling. First, close and lock all of your doors to keep yourself safe as you work on adjustments. Adjust the seat so that you are comfortable and at least 10 inches away from the steering wheel. Adjust the headrest so that it is in the middle of the back of your head. Then fasten your seatbelt and balance your hands on each side of the steering wheel. Adjust your mirrors and anything else as needed.

ADJUSTING THE MIRRORS

Alright, what does adjusting the mirrors even mean? There is, in fact, a right way and a wrong way to adjust your car's mirrors. Always adjust your mirrors from the driver's seat. Start with the rear-view mirror, and make sure that you can see the middle of your back windshield without needing to move your head. Do this after adjusting the seat so that you do not have to readjust again.

Adjust the side mirrors with the controls that are on your dashboard or your driver's side door. You should adjust the driver's side mirror so that you can see the road behind you and a small sliver of your own car, and then adjust the passenger side mirror so that it is the same way.

HOLDING THE STEERING WHEEL CORRECTLY

There is a right way and a wrong way to hold the steering wheel. Imagine the steering wheel like a clock face. Most people will tell you to hold the wheel at 10 and 2, meaning that you should put your hands at 10 o'clock and 2 o'clock on the imaginary clock face. However, for safety reasons, it is recommended that you use 9 and 3 instead.

CHANGING LANES

In order to change lanes, you will need to use your turn signal. This allows the other drivers on the road to know that you are going to change lanes. You should do this at least 100 feet before you commence to change lanes. Once your turn signal is on, check your mirrors and make sure the coast is clear. Look over your shoulder to check blindspots, and if everything seems good, then you are okay to change lanes.

KEEP DOCUMENTS IN THE CAR

Your car comes equipped with a glove box, which is the little compartment on the passenger side of the car. This is the perfect place to keep all the necessary documents. If you get pulled over, towed, or in an accident, you are going to need things like your registration, owner's manual, and any other documentation pertaining to your car on hand. The glove box is the best place to keep all of these.

DON'T TAILGATE

Make sure that you leave enough space between the car in front of you and yourself. It might seem like driving closely to someone speeds the process up or even tempts them to drive faster, but if they have to break in an emergency, you will crash into them. In fact, some drivers do something called brake checking, wherein they slam the brakes to deter tailgaters. You should never do this, but be aware that others may not extend you the same courtesy.

In this chapter, you learned all about how to keep yourself safe and satisfied in the car. Next, we'll talk about doing the same in the comfort of your own home.

WHERE YA HEADED?

Your first experiences behind the wheel are exhiliarating and you'll want to test your newfound freedom. Think about some places you intend to visit when the time comes (and with your parents permission). Where will you go? Who will you take? What kind of precautions will you need to take?

Chapter 8: Home Survival Guide

Finally, we've entered the last chapter. It is time to focus on your home and how you can maintain and deal with various problems that you may encounter. Although you still live with your parents, it never hurts to learn some of these things early on. Understanding how to care for your home can save time, thousands in repairs, and some undeserved stress down the line. You can even practice some of these in your parents' home; I'm sure they wouldn't mind a helping hand.

HOUSEKEEPING

It is so easy to avoid cleaning the house, but let me tell you about what happens when you do not maintain a strong sense of housekeeping. Within a few days, things can pile up to an unmanageable level. You'll find trash in places it doesn't belong, making you feel uncomfortable and decreasing your mental health. You'll try to clean and it will tire you out because there is so much buildup. Some people let their houses get to this condition due to depression and stress, but if you start with good housekeeping now, this can be avoided.

SETTING UP A CLEANING SCHEDULE

The first thing that you need to do is set up a cleaning schedule that works for you. Some people have daily, weekly, monthly, and/or yearly schedules, and my recommendation is that you have a combination of all of them. If it can be done within five minutes or deals with dishes and trash, it is a good rule to handle it every day. Doing laundry and scrubbing counters can be done weekly, while deep cleaning can be a monthly affair. Although, this is going to depend on you and how you personally live within your space.

Something I recommend is dedicating 25 minutes a day to cleaning. For each day of the week, focus on one room of the house and try to get 25 minutes of general cleaning done. At the end of that day, if you have more cleaning that needs to be done or notice that you have a bigger cleaning project on your hands, then you can reevaluate and schedule a time for a bigger cleaning project. Write down your cleaning goals for each day as needed and try your best to stick to them.

HOW TO CLEAN THE TOILET

Gross, I know, but the best way to keep the toilet from being the grossest place in the house is to clean it regularly. Cleaning the toilet is easy. You should start by pouring a toilet-specific cleaner around the inside of the toilet bowl, allowing it to drip from the top to the water inside the bowl. Let this sit while you work on the outside of the toilet. Spray the outside of the toilet and wipe it down with a paper towel or cleaning rag, then wipe the seat. Be sure to get the lid, the seat itself, and underneath the seat as well. Finally, with your toilet brush, scrub the inside of the toilet from the top to the bottom, and then give it a good flush. Voila! You now have a sparkly clean toilet.

LAUNDRY

Every teen eventually has to make the transition into doing their own laundry. It is better to do it now than the time you get to college, as this will only serve to make the transition to college life more confusing.

USING THE WASHING MACHINE

There are two main types of washing machines that you will encounter—a top-loading washer and a front-loader washer. As the names suggest, the type depends on if you put the clothes into the top or the front of the machine. Both operate similarly with their own intricacies. Generally, however, you can wash your clothes all the same in both.

Before you put your clothes in, separate whites, dark colors, and light colors, as well as delicate clothing, from each other. Everything is going to need to be washed separately. Then, you need to make sure you do not have anything in the pockets of your clothes, as washing tissues or money is absolutely no fun. Put your clothes into the machine and do not overfill it. You should be able to fit your hand between the opening and the clothes in your machine. Overfilling the machine can cause it to go off balance and potentially flood your laundry room.

Next, you are going to need to use detergent and fabric softener. Follow the instructions provided on the bottles in order to know how much of each to put into the machine as well as where to put it. Close the machine, select your wash cycle, and start the machine. This may go a bit differently depending on what brand and type of washing machine you have, but this part is generally self-explanatory once you take a look at the machine. If you are in doubt, ask your parents.

USING THE DRYER

The big thing to note here is that not all clothes can go in the dryer. Check the tags on everything to know how and if you can dry your clothes before you try to do so. Otherwise, you may ruin some of your favorite articles of clothing. Once you are sure you can dry your clothes, load the dryer, pick your cycle, and let it go to work. Again, consult your parents if anything is confusing to you.

IRONING CLOTHES

A lot of teens think ironing is outdated until they reach adulthood and realize how unprofessional it looks to show up in clothing that has clearly been wadded up in the back of the closet for two years. This is why you need to know the basics of ironing, even if you do not think you will ever iron a thing in your life.

In order to iron your clothes, they're going to need to be clean at first. With your clean clothes on hand, set up your ironing board. Yes, this is necessary; irons can ruin countertops. Check the labels of your clothes for ironing settings and then preheat the iron by turning it on and letting it sit with the metal part perpendicular to the board. Usually, irons have something like a heel that you can tilt back onto to let the iron sit upright. While your iron is heating, turn your clothes inside out and lay them flat. Then, spray the clothes with water unless your iron comes with a spray function. If it does, you will need to fill the iron up before you plug it in.

Then, you are going to apply the iron to your clothing. Pass the iron across the fabric slowly, one side at a time. Be careful never to let a hot iron sit for long on clothing; otherwise, you may burn the clothes or even start a fire. Once you've ironed one side, flip the garment and do the same thing to the other side. Unplug your iron and let it cool before putting it away, and you are finished! Well done.

COOKING

There's nothing like a home-cooked meal, but unfortunately, your mom or dad won't always be there to cook for you. It can also be a great way to show appreciation if you cook for them from time to time, making it really necessary to learn to cook your own food as a teen.

SIMPLE RECIPES TO MEMORIZE

You can cook whatever you want, but to get you started, I've compiled four simple recipes you can cook yourself.

CHILI MAC AND CHEESE

Ingredients

- 1 cup shredded cheese

- 11 ounces drained whole kernel corn

- 30 ounces chili with beans

- 1 small chopped onion

- 1 small chopped green pepper

- 1 pound ground beef

- 1 cup uncooked elbow pasta

Steps

1. Cook the macaroni pasta according to the instructions provided on the package and then drain the water.

2. While this cooks, crumble the beef with the chopped vegetables into a large skillet and cook on medium heat for five to seven minutes. Drain any excess liquid.

3. Stir the other ingredients together and then sprinkle the cheese on top.

And you are done! It is that simple to cook a delicious meal.

FRO-YO POPSICLES

Ingredients

- 10–3 ounce plastic cups, or 10 popsicle molds
- 1 cup fresh mixed berries
- 2 tablespoons sugar
- 2 ¾ cup honey Greek yogurt
- ¼ cup water
- 10 wooden popsicle sticks, or popsicle molds

Steps

1. Fill each cup about a quarter of the way with yogurt.

2. Put the berries, water, and sugar in a food processor and pulse until the berries are chopped finely.

3. Place about a tablespoon and a half of this mixture into each cup, then swirl with the popsicle stick.

4. Cover the cops with tin foil, and insert the sticks through the foil.

5. Place them in the freezer until they're popsicles.

PEPPERONI CROISSANT ROLLS

Ingredients

- 1 tube of crescent rolls
- 16 pepperoni slices cut into fourths
- 2 pieces of string cheese cut into fourths
- ¾ teaspoon Italian seasoning
- ¼ teaspoon garlic salt

Steps

1. Preheat the oven.

2. Unroll the dough and separate it into eight triangles.

3. Place eight pieces of pepperoni on each.

4. Set a piece of string cheese on the side of the triangle that is shortest, and then sprinkle with a half teaspoon of Italian seasoning.

5. Roll the crescents starting from the short side and pinch the seams.

6. Sprinkle with the remaining seasonings.

7. Place the rolled up crescents two inches apart on a baking sheet that has been greased and cook for ten minutes at 375.

Tasty Cherry Smoothie

Ingredients

- 1 ½ cup unsweetened apple juice
- 1 cup frozen dark sweet cherries, pitted
- 1 cup unsweetened raspberries, frozen
- 1 ½ cup raspberry sherbet

Simply combine all of the ingredients into a blender and blend well.

KITCHEN SAFETY

One of the easiest places to get hurt is in the kitchen. That means it is time for some kitchen safety tips:

- Watch what you are cooking at all times. Don't leave the kitchen to go do something else while you are cooking.

- Keep your food on the back burner; you will be less likely to harm yourself.

- Use pot holders to remove hot food, even from the microwave.

- When you microwave food, stir it to ensure that the food cooks evenly.

- Make sure that your fire extinguisher and smoke detectors are in working condition.

- Don't let pot handles hang over the edge of the stove; this is the easiest way to bump them and spill food.

- Don't eat hot food in your lap; always eat on a hard surface.

HOME REPAIR

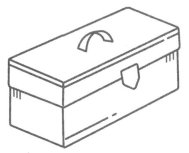

You do not want to be an adult who has to call a repair person for every little thing that goes wrong in your home. This can be both embarrassing and costly, and it doesn't have to be—most home repairs are relatively easy to conduct on your own, as you will learn now.

CHANGING A LIGHTBULB

A lot of people do not know this, but you actually need to turn the electricity off before you change the light bulb. I actually recommend cutting the power off with the breaker to be safe. Remember that most lightbulbs are hot, so give the lightbulb about 15 minutes to cool down. Remove the old bulb, and then screw the new one in. Cut the power back on and dispose of the old bulb carefully.

In some rare cases, the threading of a lightbulb can get stuck inside of the light socket. If this happens, do not try to fix it yourself—that's a very easy way to get electrocuted. Instead, be sure to call an electrician to have the broken piece removed for you.

BASIC PLUMBING

Clogs can really put a damper on your day, especially when it comes to the toilet or the sink. But there is no reason to call a plumber to deal with a simple clog. Instead, you can learn to handle them on your own.

UNCLOGGING A TOILET

It is generally a good idea to always have a plunger on hand because they're very useful. Unclogging a toilet with a plunger is the easiest way to do so. In order to unclog your toilet, you are going to want to place the plunger in the toilet. Make sure that the plunger covers the hole in the toilet perfectly; otherwise, a seal won't form and the plunger won't work. Press down gently until you feel a bit of suction has formed. Then, gently but firmly move the handle up and down about 10 times. Remove the plunger and see if the clog is removed; if it is, the toilet should unclog and flush itself automatically or flush easily when you push the handle. If the clog isn't resolved, repeat the process until it is.

UNCLOGGING A SINK

There are a handful of ways that you can unclog a clogged sink, whether it is in the kitchen or the bathroom. You can always use the plunger to do so, but for sanitation reasons, I recommend having a separate plunger for sinks from the toilet. You can unclog the sink the same way that you unclog the toilet.

If you prefer to try another method, pour boiling water down the drain. Sometimes, this can resolve the clog easily by dislodging some of the gunk that's keeping the sink backed up. If that doesn't work, you can try Drano or a drain snake with an accompanying drain declogger, in which case you just follow the directions on the bottle.

PATCHING A HOLE IN THE WALL

Sometimes, we can accidentally knock a hole in our own wall without meaning to. Swinging a door open too fast can cause the handle to go through the wall, for example, or an unfortunately placed pushpin can cause quite the level of damage. Sometimes, when you move into an apartment, there may be a small hole in the wall if it is on the cheaper side. It can cost a lot to get one of these holes fixed… unless you do it yourself, that is.

In order to repair a hole in the wall, you are going to need a wall repair kit, which is really cheap at any home repair location. It is going to come with sandpaper, which you will use to sand down the rough edges around the hole. The kit is also going to come with mesh, which you will stick over the hole. Then, you are going to spread the spackling that comes with the kit over the mesh using the provided drywall knife. Leave this to dry overnight before adding a second layer if needed. Once the spackling is dry, you can paint over it to match the color of your wall.

FIXING SQUEAKY DOOR HINGES

In most cases, a squeaky door hinge is nothing but annoying—but that annoyance can be rather major when every time you open the door, it emanates a loud screeching sound. Fortunately, fixing these squeaky hinges is going to be one of the easiest fixes that you will have to deal with as a homeowner. The best way to fix a squeaking hinge is to use WD-40, which you can find in nearly any store that sells home supplies. Simply follow the instructions on the canister and you will do well.

However, if your hinges are destroyed and need to be replaced, that's also a simple fix. You're going to need a screwdriver and new hinges that match the size and shape of the current hinges. Carefully unscrew the old hinges and replace them one at a time. Be careful to avoid letting the door fall on you or something in your home, as well as avoid letting the door hang on just one hinge, as this can damage your brand-new hinges.

SILENCING A SQUEAKY FLOOR

It is also not terribly hard to fix a squeaky floor. This usually happens to wood floors because the boards can creak individually or against one another. The easiest among the solutions is sprinkling baby powder or baking soda onto the squeaky floorboard and rubbing it into the wood. If that doesn't work, see if you can look at the floorboard from below and look for where it gaps as someone walks over it, placing a sliver of wood in the crack. If the board is loose or bulges outward, tighten it with screws from below as well. All of these solutions are very cost-effective and should help you silence those annoying floorboards!

TIGHTENING HANDLES

Your drawers and cabinets in your house are going to have handles or knobs with which to open them. All you need to fix this is a screwdriver. There are two types of screwdrivers that you will encounter—Philip's head and flat head. Philip's-head screwdrivers will look like a plus sign, while flat-head screwdrivers will look like a minus sign. In order to tighten any handles or knobs, you will need to match the type of screwdriver to the type of screw. Once you have the right screwdriver, simply turn it clockwise in order to tighten it up. This should have you all set!

CLEANING GUTTERS

To finish off our home repairs section, let's discuss cleaning out gutters. You might want to ignore your gutters, but if you do, it can cause significant damage to the roof and surrounding areas of your home. After all, gutters are there for a reason and they're not all that hard to clean. In order to clean your gutters, you will need to get a ladder and climb up there to the gutters. Make sure that your ladder is anchored well and that you won't fall before you start your climb. Use gloves as you remove the debris by hand and drop it into a bucket down below. It is also a good idea to spray the gutters with water afterward to ensure that any clogs have been alleviated.

FIRST AID AND EMERGENCIES

It is always better to be safe than sorry. You could save a life by being prepared with some of these first aid tips.

BUILDING YOUR FIRST AID KIT

Every home should have at least one first aid kit in order to care for the guests and residents of that home. Utilize this checklist to make sure that you have everything you need for your very own home-aid kit:

- adhesive tape
- aloe vera gel
- aluminum finger splint
- antibiotic ointment
- antacids
- antihistamine, such as diphenhydramine
- antiseptic solution and towelettes
- auto-injector of epinephrine, if prescribed by your doctor
- bandage strips and "butterfly" bandages in assorted sizes
- breathing barrier (surgical mask)
- calamine lotion
- cotton balls and cotton-tipped swabs
- cough and cold medications
- disposable non-latex examination gloves, several pairs
- duct tape
- elastic wrap bandages
- eye shield or pad
- eyewash solution
- first-aid manual

- hand sanitizer

- hydrocortisone cream

- hydrogen peroxide to disinfect

- instant cold packs

- large triangular bandage (may be used as a sling)

- laxative

- medications

- non-stick sterile bandages and roller gauze in assorted sizes

- pain relievers, such as acetaminophen (Tylenol, others), ibuprofen (Advil, Motrin IB, others)

- petroleum jelly or other lubricant

- plastic bags, assorted sizes

- rubber tourniquet or 16 French catheter

- safety pins in assorted sizes

- scissors and tweezers

- sterile saline for irrigation, flushing

- super glue

- syringe, medicine cup, or spoon

- thermometer

- turkey baster or other bulb suction device for flushing wounds

WHAT TO DO IN AN EMERGENCY

It is also wise to know how to act in the case of various emergency events. This section is dedicated to teaching you how to do so:

- CPR. Usually, CPR needs certification, which I definitely recommend getting if you have the abilities. But if no one around is CPR-certified and someone is in need, what do you do? First, check for a pulse and see if there are any signs of life. If they can't respond and are struggling to breathe, start by calling the emergency number for your area. Kneel down beside them and lay them flat on a firm surface. Then, you're going to give 30 chest compressions by placing your hands in the center of your chest, moving at a rate of 100 per minute. Then, open their airway, pinch the nose shut, and take a normal breath. Seal your mouth over theirs and breathe into their mouth for about one second. Do this two times. Go back and forth between chest compressions and breaths until emergency services arrive.

- First aid for a choking toddler (also useful for other individuals). You never know when you're going to be around a small child, and it's very easy for them to choke on food, toys, or other small objects. Make sure that they're choking. If they nod to indicate that they are or cannot reply, you should help them. Have someone call 911 or the applicable emergency number. Stand behind the child and wrap your arms around their waist. Make a fist with one hand with your thumb inward, and place your fist right above their belly button. Then grab your fist with your other hand. Press into their stomach with your hands like this, using an inward and upward motion until the object comes out. This works for adults too.

- Setting a splint. In order to set a splint, support the limb and gently wrap a bandage around it. Put the padded splint along the injured limb and then secure this firmly.

- Stopping bleeding. Apply pressure on the wound with a clean cloth or tissue. Don't remove it if the blood soaks through; rather, apply more of your material to the top. Raise the limb above the heart if possible, and don't apply a tourniquet unless the bleeding is incredibly severe and direct pressure isn't helping.

- Treating a burn. Cool the burn with tap water or a cold compress. Do this for about ten minutes. Then apply Vaseline to the wound 2–3 times a day.

- Spotting a concussion. Typical signs of a concussion include balance problems, dizziness, light or sound sensitivity, confusion, and feeling sluggish after head trauma.

- Identifying signs of a stroke. This can save lives if detected. Signs of a stroke include a numb sensation in the face or any limb on one side of the body, sudden confusion or notable difficulty with speaking, sudden vision issues in one or both eyes, and sudden trouble walking or remaining balanced.

And now you know how to keep yourself both comfortable and safe in your own home, from cooking to first aid.

What's in Your Toolbox?

Having a basic toolbox comes in handy in any home. You never know what small repairs or modifications you may need to take care of, but you won't be able to without a properly put together tookbox. Use this space to list out the basic tools and supplies you would keep in your own toolbox.

Conclusion

Your teenage years are some of the most interesting and confusing years of your life, which is why it is so important to find resources like this book that can help you out. Every day, teens like you struggle with some of the things you've learned throughout the course of this book, but we're slowly working to change the way teens navigate life every day.

Keeping your mind and body strong, dedicating time to what you love, working hard, acing school, and being mature about finances, as well as understanding how to care for some of your more expensive belongings like a home and a car, are the top priorities you should be focusing on. Because you've learned all of these skills and tactics to survive your teen years, I promise things are going to be smooth(er) sailing from here. Each chapter in this book has brought you one step closer to independence and self-sufficiency, and I know you will do great things with this resource.

Your teenage years are no walk in the park, but now that you are equipped with the necessary skills to not only survive but thrive during this crucial phase in your life, you have the power to shape your future and unlock your full potential! If this book was able to teach you something new or help you overcome the struggles of adolescence, then help someone else become the best version of themselves by writing us a review.

Now you have everything that you need to knock your teen years out of the park. Get out there and do great things! I believe in you.

References

Consent. (2016, February 2). Teen Health Source. https://teenhealthsource.com/sex/consent/

5 simple tips to make friends. (2015, March 3). Health for Teens. https://www.healthforteens.co.uk/relationships/friendships/5-simple-tips-to-make-friends/

Hartney, E. (2022, October 6). What is peer pressure? Verywell Mind; Verywellmind. https://www.verywellmind.com/what-is-peer-pressure-22246

How teens can be and pick a good friend. (2011, January 10). Middle Earth. https://middleearthnj.org/2011/01/10/how-teens-can-be-and-pick-a-good-friend/

How to change a flat tire. 2021. Bridgestone. https://www.bridgestonetire.com/learn/maintenance/how-to-change-a-flat-tire/

Jordan, T. (2019, January 14). The 7 best budgeting methods. Atypical Finance. https://www.atypicalfinance.com/7-best-budgeting-methods/

Markway, B. (2018, September 20). Why self-confidence is more important than you think. Psychology Today. https://www.psychologytoday.com/us/blog/shyness-is-nice/201809/why-self-confidence-is-more-important-you-think

Morin, A. (2020, June 29). 10 signs your teen is stressed out. Verywell Mind; Verywellmind. https://www.verywellmind.com/signs-your-teen-is-stressed-out-2611336

Mozafaripour, S. (2020, January 30). 10 effective study tips and techniques to try this year | USAHS. University of St. Augustine for Health Sciences. https://usa.edu/blog/study-techniques/

Running strategies for children and teens. (n.d.). HPRC. Retrieved June 19, 2023, from https://www.hprc-online.org/social-fitness/family-optimization/running-strategies-children-and-teens#:~:text=Running%20duration%20 should%20be%20no

Gray, Kurt. n.d. The keys to defensive driving. https://kidshealth.org/en/teens/ driving-safety.html

University of St. Augustine for Health Sciences. (2019, October 3). 9 popular time management techniques and tools. University of St. Augustine for Health Sciences. https://www.usa.edu/blog/time-management-techniques/

Made in the USA
Las Vegas, NV
04 December 2024

13353816R00063